PERIMETERS OF LIGHT

Discerning Biblical Boundaries for the Emerging Church

ELMER L. TOWNS
AND ED STETZER

© Copyright 2018 – Elmer L. Towns and Ed Stetzer

All rights reserved. This book is protected by the copyright laws of the United States of America. This book may not be copied or reprinted for commercial gain or profit. The use of short quotations or occasional page copying for personal or group study is permitted and encouraged. Permission will be granted upon request. Unless otherwise identified, Scripture quotations are taken from the Holy Bible, New Living Translation. Copyright © 1996, 2004, 2007 by Tyndale House Foundation. Used by permission of Tyndale House Publishers, Inc., Carol Stream, Illinois 60188. All rights reserved. Scripture quotations marked KJV are taken from the King James Version. Scripture quotations marked NIV are taken from THE HOLY BIBLE, NEW INTERNATIONAL VERSION®. Copyright © 1973, 1978, 1984, 2011 by Biblica, Inc.™ Used by permission. All rights reserved worldwide. Scripture quotations marked NASB are taken from the NEW AMERICAN STANDARD BIBLE®. Copyright © 1960, 1962, 1963, 1968, 1971, 1972, 1973, 1975, 1977, 1995 by The Lockman Foundation. Used by permission. Scripture quotations marked NKJV are taken from the New King James Version. Copyright © 1982 by Thomas Nelson, Inc. Used by permission. All rights reserved. Scripture quotations marked ESV are taken from The Holy Bible, English Standard Version. ESV® Text Edition: 2016. Copyright © 2001 by Crossway Bibles, a publishing ministry of Good News Publishers. All emphasis within Scripture quotations is the author's own. Please note that Destiny Image's publishing style capitalizes certain pronouns in Scripture that refer to the Father, Son, and Holy Spirit, and may differ from some publishers' styles. Take note that the name satan and related names are not capitalized. We choose not to acknowledge him, even to the point of violating grammatical rules.

DESTINY IMAGE® PUBLISHERS, INC.
P.O. Box 310, Shippensburg, PA 17257-0310
"Promoting Inspired Lives."

This book and all other Destiny Image and Destiny Image Fiction books are available at Christian bookstores and distributors worldwide.

For more information on foreign distributors, call 717-532-3040.
Or reach us on the Internet: www.destinyimage.com
ISBN 13 TP: 978-0-7684-4631-9
ISBN 13 EBook: 978-0-7684-4632-6

Previously published by Moody Publishers.

For Worldwide Distribution, Printed in the U.S.A.
1 2 3 4 5 6 / 21 20 19 18

Contents

Introduction: Safety and Comfort Within the Perimeter of Light v

Introduction: Taking Fire into the Jungle 1

Chapter 1: What Makes Something Christian? 5
Most everyone knows the difference between light and darkness, but what is the boundary between them? When does a Christian leave the edge of light and enter the world of darkness?

Chapter 2: Examining the Difference of Meanings and Forms 19
The chapter points out that many decisions in Christian ministry are based on preference and culture, not biblical truth. It points out our own biases, then uses cross-cultural examples to illustrate the point.

Chapter 3: Looking for Boundaries of Practice 25
What is the perimeter between true evangelism and non-biblical evangelism? How can we face many issues in today's Christian church, i.e., compromised doctrine, pseudo-miracles, entertainment-evangelism, ministry driven by the bottom-line, eroding standards of holiness, and various manifestations in revivals?

Chapter 4: What is a Church? 35
What is needed for a church to be a church? Does a church need a building? Are house churches appropriate? What functions must be present for a church to be an authentic New Testament church? Some assemblies were vibrant New Testament churches, but now they have lost their New Testament integrity. What made them lose their authenticity, i.e., what made them die?

Chapter 5: When is Worship Christian? 45
When is worship not Christian? Many people are using many different expressions to worship God, i.e., charismatic practices, secular music, dramatic presentation, etc. What worship magnifies God, and what worship does not?

Chapter 6: What Music Christian? 59
What makes music Christian? What some Christian young adults like, the older generation rejects; and other youth reject any music that's not contemporary.

Chapter 7: Looking for Biblical Preaching. 75
What makes a sermon a biblically faithful? How much Bible reference is needed? How does the preacher plan a structure for the message?

Chapter 8: When Evangelism is No Longer Christian 89

What is the nature of communicating the message of Christianity? How do we examine the spiritual qualifications of the communicator, the channel, the method, and the motives of sharing the gospel?

Chapter 9: Doing Christianity in a Postmodern World 107

The chapter is a discussion of what happens when people go too far in doctrine, practice, and judgment.

Chapter 10: The Perimeter of Truth 119

The chapter addresses what truth is. How does the postmodern world determine what truth is? Why is that wrong? How do we stand for truth in a postmodern world?

Epilogue 137

Introduction

SAFETY AND COMFORT WITHIN THE PERIMETER OF LIGHT

A Parable

Two missionaries are heading toward their mission field; the work provides challenges beyond their imagination... strategies and methods were so very clear to them in their early days. Their plan was so precise. Now, it seems as if they are off the map, both geographically and personally. Evangelism is still their dream and passion, now everything looks different.

Two sweaty missionaries are traveling through the sultry primeval jungle. They are heading for the Nimo tribe in the Sepik River Valley. Their task is simple—to evangelize this unreached tribe. As darkness began to fall, they began pitching camp for the night. The older wiser missionary began searching for firewood, stacking it at the center of the campfire.

"Why so much wood?" the younger missionary asked. "It's hot here in the jungle; we don't need a big fire."

"We'll need a fire when the night comes." He then built a fire in the center of their camp—a big fire. The younger missionary was skeptical,

"Why do we need such a large fire?"

The wiser missionary smiled because he knew what happened in the jungle at night. He answered, "The fire keeps dangerous animals and snakes away."

The younger man prepared his bedroll, but fear of the darkness gripped him as the night closed in about them. It began to get chilly. The fire comforted them and protected them. "I need a drink of water and the stream is in the darkness," he told the jungle-wise missionary. The older man knew what to do,

"Take light with you," he said. "Take enough light to keep you safe to get there and back." The older man then observed, "It's dangerous if your light goes out."

The younger man was careful to do his chores within the light of the fire, and when he was ready for sleep; he lay down as close as he could to the light. He felt safe within the perimeter of light.

During the night, the fire burned low. The perimeter of light shrank the circle around the camp. The chilly night breeze awakened him. He heard the howl of a predator in the darkness; its roar seemed closer than before. Although he couldn't see into the shadows, he felt the snakes getting closer; the hair on the back of his neck stood up. He was glad to get out of his bedroll to put more fuel upon the fire.

This book examines the fading light of the gospel in American churches. Is the Christian light of the American culture fading, or is it the light within the church that is fading? We're not living in the pitch-blackness of heathendom, nor are we living in the pure light of past awakenings. We're living in the PERIMETER OF LIGHT.

We will look at the perimeter and how to recognize it. We will examine how that perimeter expands and contracts. Hopefully, this will both challenge and cause you to think about what is light and what is personal preference. Most importantly, it will help you to consider how to take this unchanging light into an ever-changing world—doing what light does best—informing and transforming.

INTRODUCTION

Taking Fire into the Jungle

Every culture and every age presents a challenge for each community of faith. What is acceptable? What is scriptural? Answering these questions has never been an easy task. The purpose of this book is to provide a framework that will help you make those determinations in your setting. This will help you become biblically faithful as well as culturally relevant. This will help you discover relevant biblical boundaries in a sometimes-chaotic world.

Ultimately, this book is about a theology of methodology. Our intent is to help you think biblically about issues of practice and ministry. We do not provide all the answers because the answers will come, not from us, but from your interaction with the Word of God applied in your setting. But, ultimately, the book will have been successful if you and your church leaders have studied and prayed through the issues we address.

As we develop this framework, the parable of the Nimo, a tribal people in Papua New Guinea will help us illustrate the tension that exists in the struggle to determine "perimeters of the light." The issues discussed in the parable are real issues addressed by real missionaries. However, the missionaries and their stories are fictitious—a compilation of international mission experiences. However, the thought processes used by international missionaries as they contextualize the gospel will shine light upon the need for proper contextualization in North America today.

To learn more about real missionaries working among the real Nimo, visit www.Nimotribe.org. This unreached people group needs your prayers.

Taking the Gospel to the Nimo
A Parable

The missionaries were preparing to leave the safety of the missionary compound to head into the heart of the jungle. Their task was to evangelize a tribe of the Nimo that had never heard the Gospel. The trip was treacherous. Predators and diseases awaited them on their journey. Even worse, the natives that they were going to evangelize were vicious. They had killed anyone attempting to make contact with them.

The older missionary had spoken with several Nimo natives who had left the jungle tribe and were now "civilized." These tribesmen told the older missionary how to live in the jungle—where to camp and how to sleep safely in the jungle. They gave him a map that would safely guide them to the local tribe, but what will happen when they make contact with the hostile tribe?

The younger missionary was wide-eyed and optimistic. He was ready to preach the Gospel and see natives converted to Jesus Christ. He had a vision of building a church in the village with a cross. He wanted to translate the Scriptures into the native language. Above all, he wanted the church to have indigenous leadership where trained native leaders pastored the natives in that region.

"Don't get the cart before the horse," the older missionary advised him. "There are a lot of things we must do correctly to get there safely." The older and wiser missionary knew they had to take it one day at a time, and each step had to be carefully planned.

"Don't forget to take matches," the older missionary's voice had a fearful tone. "We must build a fire each night . . ." his voice trailed off into nothing. The veteran missionary knew a fire would protect them at night. "We will be safe within the perimeter of light."

The older missionary told how a fire was warm and comfortable. He had spent a terrifying night without a fire and did not want to go through that experience again. Then the older missionary continued with instructions for his younger companion,

"Never go into the jungle without fire." By that statement he meant the ability to make fire. "When the jungle is menacingly dark, we will be protected by the perimeter of light."

Christian ministry no longer involves living simply and safely in one North American town, just preaching, serving, and doing "safe" things.

Effective ministry no longer involves drinking afternoon tea with the ladies auxiliary or going out to lunch with board members. It is no longer just preaching packaged sermons and performing weddings and funerals.

The North American Church is now on a mission field. Over the last few decades, the church in North America has lost the home field advantage. Today, we are living in a jungle of lostness, not a religious society that looks to us for leadership.

Pastors are being attacked and crippled for ministry. Some are driven out of ministry altogether. The reputation of God is being "dragged through the mud." The glory of God is equated with pulpit or healing sensationalism. Evangelism is equated with being non-offensive, non-confrontational, or tolerant of other religious ways of 'salvation.'

As the two missionaries prepare to evangelize a tribe of hostile natives, they must take into consideration the dangers they face from those they desire to reach. Lost people are often hostile to the gospel, and the issue has to be addressed.

People in ministry also have to consider the environment around them. They need to take the light into the darkness, and the darkness envelopes certain dangers. They could stay in the compound. That is where it is safe. They could stay by the fire. That is certain and comfortable. However, their task is to take the light into the darkness without being consumed by that darkness.

We are not just called to be the light. We are also called to send the light—or, perhaps more accurately, to be sent as the light. As a result, it is necessary for us to continually press on toward the very edge of light and darkness. It is upon that edge where the power of God becomes most evident—bringing those from darkness to the light. If we only stay in the comfort of the light, we have become like spiritual Amish, isolated and insulated while the darkness has free reign.

Each chapter of this book will expand upon the parable of the Nimo. Each segment is intended to grab your attention and provoke your thoughts. As you read this book with a group of other believers, use the parable to stimulate discussion. Stories can help us to grasp deeper truths. We hope the parable will help you clearly grasp the issues Christianity faces.

In our society, calls for tolerance surround us. Many sincere Christians hear their friends say "all religions lead to God," and they halfway believe,

"All you have to be is sincere—believe with all your heart." They question, "Is Jesus the only way to Heaven?"

The basic premise of this book is *argument ad absurdum*, i.e., truth is seen when both issues are pressed to the opposite extreme. A Christian stands in pure light, and the closer to God he or she gets, the purer the light becomes. He or she is transformed by the light and then becomes a source of that light.

Non-Christians are spiritually blind and stand in absolute darkness. A lost person cannot understand spiritual things apart from God. The problem is that many Christians want to stand with one foot in the light and one foot in the darkness. They stand in the "twilight zone" on the perimeter of light.

> *This is the message which we have heard from Him and declare to you, that God is light and in Him is no darkness at all. If we say that we have fellowship with Him, and walk in darkness, we lie and do not practice the truth. But if we walk in the light as He is in the light, we have fellowship with one another, and the blood of Jesus Christ His Son cleanses us from all sin* (John 1:5-7).

Our hope is that this book will help you walk in the light while pushing back the darkness. We give thanks for those who have held out the light so that we could come to Jesus Christ, the Light of the World. We give thanks for many Bible teachers who have shined the light of the Word in our life.

Thanks also to my (Elmer) assistant, Linda Elliott, who edited and typed this manuscript through its many revisions. Thanks to Dino, Jeff, Mike, Chris, Betty, and Lizette who are always faithful readers of my (Ed) writings. Finally, we appreciate the patience of the staff of Moody Press in working with this manuscript.

We give thanks to many, but take all the responsibility for the weakness and omissions of this manuscript. May it accomplish much in the lives of many.

Sincerely yours in Christ,
Elmer L. Towns and Ed Stetzer

Chapter 1

WHAT MAKES SOMETHING CHRISTIAN?

A Parable

The younger missionary was surprised at how many Nimo were wearing a cross. They were now friendly and were coming around the missionary compound. The younger missionary said, "It seems like everybody I saw was wearing a cross. I thought the Nimo were not Christians."

The older missionary explained, "Among the Nimo, there are lots who are 'Christians' and lots who act like Christians. They pray to their ancestors, keep charms to protect them, and pray to Jesus to forgive their sins. They have some light but have not left the darkness."

"Let's get everyone who is not a Christian to take off the cross," the young missionary said. He reasoned that way they could tell who was a Christian.

The older missionary had another idea, "Maybe wearing a cross will help them become a Christian quicker."

"Suppose they don't become a Christian," the younger missionary said.

"Suppose they do," the older one replied.

Where is the perimeter of light located? It's hard to determine where light stops and darkness begins. Light gently fades into night. Actually, the perimeter is not located at an exact spot, because if the fire burned brighter, the edge expands and enlarges the circle of protection. When the fire is almost out, the perimeter is so small it becomes almost too small to provide protection for one human. The perimeter of light changes according to the brightness of the fire.

The edge of light is not a line drawn in the night. The energy of the fire determines how far the light reaches into a darkened night. The flickering flames of a fire make the edge dance; the edge dashes out into the darkness when the flame sparkles or flickers brightly. The edge creeps hesitantly away from the darkness backwards towards the campers when they allow the fire to die.

The edge of light between Christianity and the world is not a distinct boundary line that can always be easily seen. It is a perimeter. Even though we see gray areas in Christianity, nothing is gray to God. We don't see things the way God sees them. God knows what is Christian and what is not Christian, even when it's blurry to us. Christianity is not a religion, like joining a movement. Being a Christian means having a relationship with Christ. Christianity is about that relationship between God and His people.

If Christianity were a "religion," it would have boundaries as other world religions of the world. You would do certain things and that would qualify you as a Christian. But Christianity does not have a fence to keep people in—or keep them out. Although it does have principles by which a person should keep in relationship with God, Christianity is not a set of rules that you have to keep to become or remain a Christian, although it does have principles by which you live for God. Christianity is about a person; it is about Jesus Christ, and if you are properly related to Him by faith, you're a Christian. The light is Jesus, and the edge determines tells how close to Jesus you live.

The perimeter is not a boundary where the traveler passes from total light to total darkness. A perimeter is a "twilight zone" where it's not completely light, nor is it completely black. Sometimes it's hard to see clearly in the edge zone, and it's hard to see the edge itself. God knows where Christianity leaves off and the world takes over. Even when you are not sure where the boundary is located, God knows.

The Difference between Edges and Boundaries

Webster's Dictionary has defined boundary as "something that indicates or fixes a limit," i.e., a separating line. The emphasis is on the actual point that separates two items or views. If you apply the concept of boundaries to Christianity, there are fences or property lines between Christianity and non-Christianity. *The Oxford Dictionary* adds the following definition to *boundary*, "That which must be limited, confined or restrained." This means Christianity is limited or bound up. Therefore, the nature of Christianity would demand limits.

There are some boundaries that relate to practice:

- There is a line between an authentic church (Matt. 16:18) and a group that only has the title "church," but is not a true church in God's sight (Rev. 2:12-29).
- There is a difference between true worship (John 4:20-24) and activities that take place in a church but are not true worship—they may even be anti-worship (Colossians 2:16-23).
- There is music that points people to God (2 Chronicles 5:11-14) and music that does not (Isaiah 14:11-15).
- Somewhere between biblical principles of biblical evangelism (Matt. 28:19, 20) and human methods (Matt. 7:26-27), there are practices that a church should not use in evangelism.
- Somewhere there is a boundary between the true manifestation of the Holy Spirit (Acts 2:1-4) and a false spirit that only mimics Christianity (Acts 8:19-23). Sometimes the spirit is an evil spirit that attempts to imitate the Holy Spirit (Acts 19:13-16).

Certain boundaries of practice can also lead to error. What we do does impact what we believe. Somewhere in the journey from true Christianity (1 Tim. 3:16) to heresy (1 Tim. 1:19, 20), you cross a point of no return, i.e., a boundary or property line. God's property is located on one side of the fence; Satan's property is on the other side. Somewhere in a journey from holiness (1 Peter 1:16) to ungodliness (2 Peter 2:21-22), there is a boundary line beyond which a person should not step.

The study of boundaries is not a new challenge, nor is it a new reaction. There were questions even in the early church as to where the fences should be built. John wrote,

"Dear friends, do not believe every spirit, but test the spirits to see whether they are from God, because many false prophets have gone out into the world" (1 John 4:1).

Jude wrote,

> *"For certain men whose condemnation was written about long ago have secretly slipped in among you. They are godless men, who change the grace of our God into a license for immorality and deny Jesus Christ our only Sovereign and Lord"* (Jude 4).

Peter warned,

> *"But there were also false prophets among the people, just as there will be false teachers among you. They will secretly introduce destructive heresies, even denying the sovereign Lord who bought them—bringing swift destruction on themselves. Many will follow their shameful ways and will bring the way of truth into disrepute"* (2 Peter 2:1-2).

Paul warned,

> *"The Spirit clearly says that in later times some will abandon the faith and follow deceiving spirits and things taught by demons"* (1 Tim. 4:1).

It seems every generation has always battled with the boundaries issue. Most boundary debates involved doctrinal issues, but not all. Some were boundary issues of methodology—, or "how to express Christianity." Martin Luther rejected the enthusiasts. John Wesley was ridiculed for his new "methods" and was sarcastically labeled "Methodist." Jonathan Edwards struggled with emotional expressions of revivalism in the First Great Awakening, and Charles Finney was criticized for embracing "the right use of appropriate means" in the Second Great Awakening. With each new outreach of the gospel, new methods have emerged. Reactions to the new methods are usually negative.

The very nature of Christianity implies that there would be an on-going battle to keep the church pure. Satan is called "a liar" (John 8:44). Originally, he distorted God's Word in the Garden of Eden. Is it not plausible that he would distort God's Word and God's methods today? The Adversary still attempts to corrupt the minds of believers (1 Cor. 11:3) and blinds the minds of non-believers (2 Cor. 4:3, 4).

God divinely knew there would be attempts to both dilute His message and to add to it. While the following was a direct reference from the last book of the Bible, the meaning can be applied to all Scriptures—.

"I warn everyone who hears the words of the prophecy of this book: If anyone adds anything to them, God will add to him the plagues described in this book.

And if anyone takes words away from this book of prophecy, God will take away from him his share in the tree of life and in the holy city, which are described in this book" (Rev. 22:18, 19).

For some, it is easy to draw hard edges. Some groups believe that they are the only correct church—and all others are in error. However, this makes little sense. Obviously, there are Christians that differ from us, and they are still Christians. The question is how far can one be from the light and still be a Christian.

So, it is obvious that the task is difficult, and the answers will not be perfect. As a result, few are addressing the issue from the center of evangelicalism. However, it is an essential need.

When dealing with an "edge" related to Christianity, a common problem is the creation of false boundaries—boundaries that are culturally conditioned but are not biblically required. It is important to know the difference.

The Edge of Error

The edge of error is to be avoided at all times. The purpose of the Christian, church, and denomination is to stay as far away from the perimeter of error as possible. Yet, there must also be recognition that although we think we are as far from error as possible, there are other Christians who are wrong about some things but are still Christian brothers and sisters.

What does it mean to be "wrong" or "in error?" In today's world, people object to the idea that someone is right or wrong. We will address this issue on a deeper level later. However, initially let us say that many Christians are wrong about certain things. Not everyone can be right. Either the Bible teaches that all true believers will persevere until the end or it does not; either speaking in tongues is the initial evidence of the baptism of the Holy Spirit, or it is not. Both cannot be right.

The idea that the Bible can mean anything based on the response of the reader actually devalues the Word of God and destroys Christian unity. If the Bible can mean anything, then it really means nothing. Instead, the authors of scripture had specific truths in mind when they wrote the scripture text. They are either rightfully interpreted correctly, or they are wrongfully interpreted incorrectly. Some Christians are right, and some are wrong.

The problem is determining which Christians are right and which are wrong? In the New Testament era, there was already confusion. That confusion continues today. There are 38,000 denominations in the world today. All of them can't be right.

Although some are wrong and some are right, we are unwise to think that we are always the "right" ones. On the one hand, we should THINK we are right. Even the world acknowledges that all religions think they are right. Just this week, I (Ed) saw CNN's Larry King question a Methodist Bishop who implied that Christianity was not the only way to God.[1] (The United Methodist news service, in a story, distanced itself from the comments of Bishop Talbert and wrote "United Methodists believe faith in Jesus Christ is the only way the Bible gives to salvation and heaven."[2])

Both of the authors (Elmer and Ed) came to Christ in other denominations and determined that they were wrong about certain doctrines—we both became Baptists because of what Baptists believed. We thought (and still think) that our denomination is the closest we can find to a correct right interpretation of scripture.

However, we are pretty sure that some of the things we believe will be corrected when we get to heaven. (We don't know which—if we knew that we would change!) There are just too many Christians who differ on too many issues for us to be sure we have every doctrinal distinctive correct. Yet, for now, we think they are wrong (or else we would hold their views).

So, if edges are important, then the question of HOW wrong is essential. Charismatics can be wrong (or Baptists, if you are a charismatic!), but they are still our brothers and sisters in Christ. Yet, Mormons are not. What about Catholics? What about Liberal Protestants?

The diagram below will attempt to illustrate the "edge." We do so with great trepidation. Who are we? Why do we get to judge? Well, we do not. Ultimately, only God can make the determination of who is faithful and who is not. Yet, there is a tremendous need to look at this issue today. Our hope is that the diagram below will help you to discuss these edges.

---

1. CNN, Larry King Live, "Panel of Christians Speaks Out on War with Iraq," Transcript, aired March 11, 2003 - 21:00 ET, http://www.cnn.com/TRANSCRIPTS/0303/11.

2. United Methodist News Service, "Religious leaders debate war on 'Larry King Live'," March 12, 2003, http://umns.umc.org/03/mar/137.htm.

The issue may seem unimportant—unless you are part of a church or a denomination struggling with the issues. The issue of the "edge" is on the front page of Presbyterian, Methodist, and Anglican churches around the world. For those of us outside of these communities, the issue is also important—it frames how we will relate to these groups and others.

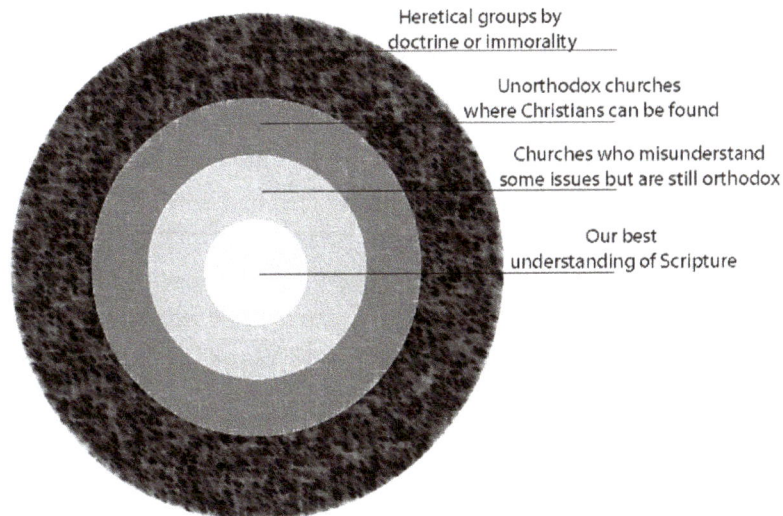

Many of our brothers and sisters are wrestling with the issues every day. A few examples:

- The Anglican Church is gripped in a worldwide struggle for what is evangelical while some third-world bishops are sending missionaries to the United States calling the Episcopal Church here an apostate church. (and several dioceses in the states are formally agreeing with the third-world bishops; asking to be placed under their authority and out from the US Episcopal Church.) Some synods are ordaining homosexuals while its most problematic retired Bishop (James Spong of New Jersey) asks if Jesus was a homosexual.

- The Confessing Movement of the Methodist Church is struggling to return the church to an evangelical conviction.
- The Evangelical Theological Society addressed (in its annual meeting, 2002) the boundary of evangelicalism itself, rejecting as heresy the idea of Open-theism (the idea that God does not know the future).

For many of you reading this book, the "edge" may seem to be too abstract to consider, but for others, this book is about a life and death struggle.

Throughout history, groups have always needed to define their edges. In some cases, they did so very clearly by signifying what they believed and what they did not. For example, the Chicago Statement on Biblical Inerrancy explains in Article I: "We *affirm* that the Holy Scriptures are to be received as the authoritative Word of God. We *deny* that the Scriptures receive their authority from the Church, tradition, or any other human source" (italics added).

A Static Edge. In some cases, we have to look at what is outside of and what is inside of the edge of light. This is not an easy task, because genuine people are often misled. If the Mormon believes that she is saved by Temple rituals, it is important for us to tell the truth about conversion. She is outside the edge of light.

A Receding Edge. On the other hand, there are some who are backing away from the light—individuals, churches, and denominations that were once in the light (sometimes they were key denominations in the light), but they have gradually withdrawn from Biblical fidelity. They have receded away from the light.

Christian brothers and sisters are faced with painful decisions regarding deciding whether to leave or stay within their own churches and denominations as these entities have receded from the light. J. I. Packer wrote an explanation of his own actions (walking out of an Anglican Synod that was endorsing homosexuality).

> Why did I walk out with the others? Because this decision, taken in its context, falsifies the gospel of Christ, abandons the authority of Scripture, jeopardizes the salvation of fellow

human beings, and betrays the church in its God-appointed role as the bastion and bulwark of divine truth.[3]

Packer determined that the edge of error had been crossed and he could no longer participate.

This edge of error is essential yet elusive. How is a person to decide when others are in error? The task is not easy. The Anglican Church is

This edge of error is essential yet elusive. How is a person to decide when others are in error? The task is not easy. The Anglican Church is an example. There are biblically faithful evangelical Anglican churches around the world. As a matter of fact, the majority of Anglican churches outside the English-speaking world are Bible-believing and evangelical. But the church in England, Canada, and the United States has compromised in many ways.

Some would question why Packer did not walk out earlier—or why he is still Anglican at all (more on that later). We will examine how far is too far, but also, how we relate to those who have gone too far.

False Boundaries: The Edge of Culture

The edge of culture is different than the edge of error. The Christian needs to get as far from the edge of error as possible. Unfortunately, that is not true for the edge of culture. Instead, we need to approach the edge of culture without going too far. The question is, how far is too far?

Of course, many will strongly object to the paragraph above. Some will think that culture should never influence what we should do. I (Ed) remember attending seminary chapel one day when the speaker shouted, "We must not let the hell-bound culture determine what takes place in our churches." Lots of "Amens" were shouted. It sounded good, but it was ultimately unworkable.

You see, he was wearing a business suit (20th century culture), preaching after singing 18th century hymns, while sitting in pews that only became popular in the 15th century. He had no problem with culture influencing almost everything he did, as long as it was church culture.

If only it were so easy. If only we could all be spiritually Amish. We would never have to worry about what is appropriate in worship and why.

---

3. J. I. Packer, "Why I Walked: Sometimes Loving a Denomination Requires You to Fight," Christianity Today, January 1, 2003, http://www.christianitytoday.com/ct/2003/001/6.46.html.

We would never be concerned about what people wear. We would never have to worry about any issues of culture.

Yet, that is not our call. Our call is to take the never-changing message into an ever-changing world. Our task is to be living incarnations of this message in a new culture and place. We cannot be Biblical when we condemn culture, but neither can we be Biblical when we adopt every cultural norm. Somewhere there is a limit. Somewhere there is an edge.

The edge of culture is different because we need to go there—but not too far. Some think that there is no cultural edge that is too far to reach people for Christ. That position is as unworkable as the preacher who thinks that culture does not matter. If we adopt every value of the world in order to reach them, how are we different? Yes, lost people matter to God and we should go far to reach them. However, if we compromise in order to do such, then we destroy the very message we are seeking to proclaim.

The edges of culture are different than the edges of error. There are two edges to culture—and our job is to steer the middle course. On the one side, we are so afraid of culture that we stay far away—and the gospel is unclear and obscure. On the other side, we are so connected with the culture that there is no difference. We have become part of the culture and our faith is compromised. There are false edges on both sides.

Why go to the edge? Why not stay as close as you can to the light? That's what we do with theology—get as close as we can to a pure understanding of scripture. Why not do the same with culture? It's safe. No chance of compromise; no problem with worldliness. The Amish never have to worry about the world—they are completely safe and engaged with the light.

It is interesting to note that we are not called to stay away from the darkness. We are called to come to faith (light) and then to participate in the divine nature (2 Peter 1:4). But central to that new life is a call to go to the darkness and to bring light into the darkness.

One of the fundamental definitions of a Christian is a Christ-follower. Jesus said, "As the Father has sent me, I am sending you" (John 20:21). So, we are sent like Jesus into a dark and dying world. Jesus is called an Apostle in Hebrews (3:1). An apostle is one who is sent with a message. Jesus then says we are sent in the same manner.

We are sent—and being sent means we take the light to the darkness. In order for the lost to see the light, they must be able to understand it. This is where many people will not go. In order for the lost to understand the light, we must share our faith in ways that they can understand. We must go to connect with them through their cultural expressions.

Let us illustrate. Today, a debate is raging in the Russian Orthodox Church and among some split-off groups. For centuries, Russian Orthodox priests dressed a certain way—long black robes, beards, and a large cross. Their attire proclaimed that they were representatives of the light. Today, some priests believe that they can better share the light if they do not look so odd to the people around them.

In their attempt to proclaim the light, their very desire to avoid compromise causes the world to miss the message. It's easy to point a finger at the Russian Orthodox (after all, they do dress funny), but how many people in North America think that being a Christian means being a conservative Republican, having no facial jewelry, and having a short haircut. When becoming a Christian means changing political affiliation or changing appearance, we have created a false gospel. Coming to Christ means coming to Christ where you are and then changing as He, not we, directs!

Some will go too far in an attempt to take the light into the darkness. They will adopt too many of the values of the world around them, and they will compromise and dilute the gospel. This is technically called syncretism—when the values of the world are mixed with the true faith.

Some will not go far enough. They will wear their robes, beards, and crosses while the world considers them quaint but irrelevant. They cause the world to confuse the true faith with rules (robes, beards, political party, length of hair, etc.) This is technically called obscurantism—when rules and traditions obscure the true faith and confuse the world.

The ultimate challenge is for the church to be biblically faithful and yet to be contextual. In other words, it is an appropriate expression of the gospel in a certain context. We would expect a Korean church to look different than an African church, and both of those would look different than an Anglo church in Alabama. They can all be biblically faithful in their context while dressing differently, singing different kinds of music, and even listening to the Word preached in a different manner. They are contextual biblical churches.

However, this is never easy. The edge between the light and the darkness is always difficult to define:

> (C)ontextualization (is) a delicate enterprise if ever there was one . . . the evangelist and mission strategist stand on a razor's edge, aware that to fall off on either side has terrible consequences... Fall to the right and you end in obscurantism, so attached to your conventional ways of practicing and teaching the faith that you veil its truth and power from those who are trying to see it through very different eyes. Slip to the left and you tumble into syncretism, so vulnerable to the impact of paganism in its multiplicity of forms that you compromise the uniqueness of Christ and concoct "another gospel which is not a gospel.[4]

Therefore, the task is to go to the edge of the light but not to go too far and become like the darkness. The good news is that this makes us like Jesus. He became incarnate--He became one flesh in the world with its customs, values, music, culture, etc. Then He sent us--to incarnate the unchanging message into new customs, values, music, cultures, etc. We are to go to (or be in) the world but not be of the world. This is the edge of the light.

In the history of Christianity, there are more failures than successes. Most churches retreat into the light and refuse to make changes that will help them "send the light." Many churches look so much like the world it is hard to see the light. This book is an attempt to help you go to the edge, but not to go over it!

The edges of culture with regards to the faith might be illustrated as follows:

---

4. Dean S. Gilliland, ed., The Word Among Us (Dallas: Word Publishing, 1989), vii.

It is important to note that there are TWO errors—one on the right and one on the left. Having a church that never struggles with cultural compromise and, as a result isolates itself from reaching the world is sin—a grave sin. Yet, so is a church that compromises by selling out to its culture. There are boundaries. There is an edge of the light.

NEED FOR BOUNDARIES

There are different forces and pressures on the church today so we must re-examine our boundaries. We should not change the biblical nature of the church, nor should we change the biblical boundaries of scripture. But some of our past boundaries were not biblical. Some of our past boundaries were culturally driven, or they were fences that we erected out of fear, embarrassment or ignorance. As we grow in our understanding of Christianity, perhaps we need to reposition our boundaries.

Today, we have to think like missionaries. We need to think of North America the way we have always thought about the "pagan" world. We have to ask: how do we take the gospel into the pagan darkness that is post-Christian North America?

As the world in which we minister, the people to whom we minister, and the way in which we communicate all change, what implications does all this have on our ministry? Read on!

QUESTIONS TO CHEW ON

1. What are some ways that we go to a culture with the gospel of the light? What parts of your culture are dark and what parts can God use?

2. How do you differentiate between the edge of error and the edge of culture? How do these two edges interact with each other?

3. What are some boundaries from the past that seem "quaint" today—based on culture and not scripture?

4. In what ways is the light of the Gospel losing its brilliance in America?

5. Who is responsible for the low flickering of the light of Christianity in America?

6. What are some ways that we carry the gospel of the light into a culture's darkness?

Chapter 2

THE DIFFERENCE OF MEANINGS AND FORMS

A Parable

The missionaries started their strategy. "First, we need to teach them modesty," suggested the younger missionary. The older missionary just smiled. "Does someone have to dress a certain way to be a Christian?" he asked. "Ok, then we need to teach them not to dance," the younger missionary quickly added. "Why teach them what not to do—why not teach them to know Christ and then let Him lead them," the older missionary replied.

"Well, if they don't start reading the Bible and they don't stop dancing, how can we know if they are Christians? What will make them different?" asked the younger missionary.

The older missionary explained, "The difference will not be in the outward things. These are the things that they will change quickly and easily to please us as visitors. However, that is not really change. They need to have a heart change. They need to have an old heart replaced with a new heart. Then, all that they do will be for a different reason—and their dress and their dance will come from a new heart. That is the tricky part—we need to bring Jesus, not our western culture, dress, and worship."

The younger missionary looked puzzled and asked, "How can we tell the difference...?"

The Challenge of Meanings and Forms

The Bible has clear commands about certain cultural subjects. We are to be kind (2 Corinthians 6:1-10; Colossians 3:12), dress modestly (Jer. 4:30; Deut 22:5; Matt 6:28; 1 Titus 2:9), speak gentle words (Matthew 12:37; 2 Peter 2:3, 18), and be reverent in worship (John 4:24; Daniel 3:28) to name a few. But how do we do these things? Does the application change from place to place, culture to culture, and generation to generation? How can we establish biblical boundaries in different cultures?

At the moment I (Ed) write this, I am sitting in the back row of a church in Peru—and I am trying to decide how to apply these meanings into the culture of urban Trujillo.

Children are talking quietly during the message, but no one seems to mind. They are expected to murmur quietly. Yet, one little girl was speaking too loud. The pastor turned and looked, and soon mother and daughter were rushing out the back. I guess her voice was too loud and it became disrespectful—but how am I to know?

I am not the preacher of the evening service, so I am dressed casually. But not so for the pastor. He is the messenger of God's Word and such a messenger must be dressed appropriately for the task. He wears a suit because it is respectful in urban Trujillo—even if it is smoldering hot.

The music is too upbeat for me. A young man plays on the guitar, another bangs a box like a drum, and a young woman leads worship. The words are Spanish as well as the music style.

The people are dressed in working class clothes—which is appropriate, for that is who they are. However, it is not appropriate for the pastor to wear working class clothes. It would be disrespectful and would not give proper honor to God.

The service was scheduled to start at 7 p.m., but that particular time is rather meaningless. About half the people showed up late; no one was offended. They had respect for the office of pastor but not for the starting time of the worship service.

So many cultural issues can be identified in such a short time. This cultural example is *instructive* because it illustrates that many biblical commands are often expressed through culturally appropriate actions. (In case you are wondering, no one seems to care that this chapter is being written during the sermon.)

This is not true of all Biblical commands. We are commanded to give, not lust, be committed to Christ, etc., and these are not cultural (though they have cultural elements). Yet, modesty, respect, and worshipfulness can only be expressed through culture. They have *meaning* that can only be expressed through *form*.

Herein lies a great problem. Since certain Bible teachings (meanings) can only be expressed through cultural actions (forms), two people from different cultures express or show the meaning differently. They both hold to the meaning but have different forms. As a result, they can often develop different convictions regarding appropriate expressions of meaning.

Yet, there is no other option. Certain things are *only* expressed through form—and these forms are the *only way* we know how to show the meaning! My parents dressed up for church as a sign (form) of respect (meaning). There is no way to separate the two—because it is what they knew. They would not come to a church casually dressed; they see it as inappropriate and disrespectful.

In my part of North America, showing up late is a sign of disrespect. It shows a casual disregard for the time of another person and places oneself above others. Yet, the pastor was late to this church tonight. (Yet, he was properly dressed.) His actions would have the opposite impact at my home church—where wearing a suit and tie is not a sign of respect but showing up for the start of the service is!

It is hard to preach about meaning but easy to preach about form. "Be culturally respectful in your dress" just won't preach. "Cut your hair, take off the hat, and pull up your pants!" does. Unfortunately, the latter is legalism (form) and the former is truth (meaning).

You see, the focus on form ultimately leads to disaster—even though we love it so much. It is like the myth of the siren's song calling us to destruction. If we can get them to dress this way, show respect this way, sing this way, and love God this way, then they will be right with God. But it is a lie—and it is self-destructive because it only provides the form without the meaning—a form of godliness without the power. It leads to a faith that is only about form—superficial and phony. Such a faith is almost always rejected by the children and friends of those who hold it.

Focusing on forms always leads to the rejection of the gospel in the next generation. Going to movies was once considered a serious sin. Movie theatres were places of worldly entertainment, and Christians would not be seen in such a place. They did not go because Christians knew that they should avoid the appearance of evil (meaning), and avoiding movies showed commitment (form) to that truth (meaning). Now, the children of many "movie abstainers" have a hard time seeing the meaning—and they have just rejected the church and its legalistic form.

Obsessing over movie attendance seems quaint today. Few reading this would consider walking into a theater a sin. However, we forget the damage this emphasis on form has caused. Many believers in the '60s and '70s rejected the unreasonableness of a faith that focused on the sin of projecting light through film onto a screen. They did not understand the form and rejected it—and many eventually rejected its underlying meaning—living a holy life.

It is not easy to separate meaning and form. (I'm still in church and people keep coming in late—and it is bothering me.) Any time that someone does not follow an assumed form, we perceive that the meaning is impacted.

Making Right Choices

This is a book about choices—and how we make them. These choices will mainly be about practices—what we DO in our churches and in our ministries. Most of us choose based upon our preferences—what we find worshipful, what music seems right, what evangelism seems best, etc. Generally speaking, there is one major problem with this method—every person is different and every decision is personal.

Actually, there is more than one problem. The main problem is that, in some cases, we have a preference when God does not. Thus, our preferences are based upon ourselves—the preferences of imperfect, sinful people.

Is there a better way? Sort of. The process starts by acknowledging that God has no preferences regarding style, but highly regards motives and outcomes. This is not to say that God has no preferences, but it does mean that God has no preferred style.

Style is cultural. Some people have church at 11 a.m. on Sunday, some at 10 p.m. God doesn't care. Some use a piano, and some use a guitar. God doesn't care. Some pastors wear robes, some wear suits, some wear golf shirts. God doesn't care.

What does God care about? He cares about His glory. John Piper, in his book, **Let the Nations Be Glad,** said, "God's ultimate goal is to uphold and display the glory of his name."[5] Is He glorified at the 10 p.m. service? Is He glorified by the piano? Is He glorified by the robe? God's concern is His glory—and our concern should be the same. We should ask how to best glorify God in our content.

---

1. John Piper, Let the Nations Be Glad (Grand Rapids, MI: Baker Book House, 2003), 17.

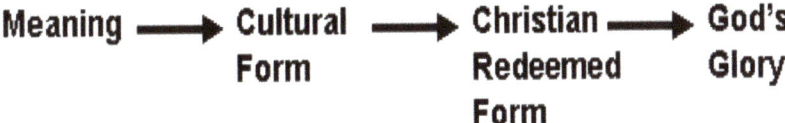

The truth may be best illustrated through the absurd. If traditional music is better, then we should be as traditional as possible. If the guitar is bad, so is the organ—come to think of it, at least the guitar is in the Bible (sort of—it is a stringed instrument!).

We should not take any risk that instruments might ignite lustful passions. But, even music is a risk—let's just read antiphonally (responsive reading back and forth). And, let's be sure that we don't read the wrong thing—let's read only scripture. Thus, if contemporary music were bad, then good "music" would have us reading the psalms aloud.

One web page (condemning all music in the church) explained, "Satan has always used sexually attractive choirs and musicians to seduce people…"[6] If contemporary music is seductive, wouldn't that also be true for choral music? Isn't the safest choice to avoid music altogether?

If women wearing pants is a problem, why not recommend a dress?—a long dress. But, that is really not enough. There needs to be absolutely no chance of worldliness—we should avoid showing any part of a leg. Women should wear a burqa as they do in the Middle East. (And men should have crew cuts to be sure their hair is not long.)

The more careful we are about avoiding these "sins" the less effective we are at evangelism. How successful will we be when we reach out with a faith of no music, men's crew cuts, and women's burqas? We would be safe from the chance of sin but unable to share Jesus with a lost world.

The reality is that we need a balance. Yes, music does stir the emotions. Yes, that can cause problems. However, we are emotional beings because God created us as such. Our task is to find the balance between using some elements of the culture without being co-opted by the culture. We need to redeem certain cultural elements and discard others. This book will help you decide which are which.

---

2. Look to the Hills Leadership and Worship Conference," accessed September 2, 2003; http://www.piney.com/Zoe-Look-To-The-Hills.html.

Moving Boundaries

Boundaries are needed, but not all boundaries are so clear. For example, which music would glorify God? Well, it depends on the culture. Music needs certain characteristics to glorify God, but those characteristics are culturally determined. On the other hand, the fact that the boundaries are moving based upon cultural differences does not mean that boundaries do not exist. On the contrary, it means we need to carefully search the scriptures and understand the culture before determining the boundaries.

QUESTIONS TO CHEW ON

1. How has your church / denomination focused on forms in the past?

2. How can we know when outward forms have lost their meaning? What should we do when they lose their meaning?

3. What are some forms that were important in the past, but have lost their meaning? Why?

4. List some things your church does that are important to it, but would not be important in a different country? What about a different generation?

5. What are some principles that will help us know when a form is no longer relevant?

6. Since Christianity is light, how have our forms caused shadows to obscure the light?

Chapter 3

BOUNDARIES OF PRACTICE

The Parable

The two missionaries were building a big fire in preparation for spending the night in the jungle. When the younger missionary headed to the stream for water, the older missionary reminded him, "Take a big torch, there are lots of snakes along that stream." Then, in an afterthought the older companion added, "The light will keep you safe."

Later that evening they discussed the practices of the young Nimo church. *The young Christians jerked their legs when singing Christian songs, just as they had jerked when worshipping their idol. The younger missionary was uncomfortable with their practice because it reminded him of demon activity.*

"The answer is light," the older missionary replied. "Just as you were protected from snakes with plenty of light when you went for water, so the new Nimo Christians will be protected from the Evil One when we give them plenty of Christian light."

Centuries of Struggles

Christians have struggled with boundaries for twenty centuries. Struggle has happened doctrinally through councils, creeds, and statements. In the second century, the church addressed the errors of inflated knowledge and out of control charismatic practices (Gnosticism and Montanism). In the fourth century, the church battled over the eternal nature of God the Son (Arianism). In the fifth century, the church had to address false teachers who taught that Jesus was not both fully God and fully man (Nestorianism). In the sixteenth century, the church battled against those who taught that we could obtain entry in to heaven through giving and works (hence the Reformation). Since the nineteenth century, the church has had to battle those who abandoned the scriptures for liberalism. The issues may change or may reoccur in a slightly altered form but the church continues to struggle today. Why would we think that our era should be free of important issues of doctrine and theology?

Great doctrinal controversies still exist today. Many denominations have adopted doctrines and practices that are not just questionable or debatable but are actually heretical. There are still some within these denominations who remain as a faithful remnant but they are struggling doctrinally.

The greatest areas of controversy are not battles from the outside, but on what practices are truly Christian and appropriate. Considerable controversy exists concerning what is appropriate in church. The seeker-sensitive movement of the 80s and 90s was (and remains) controversial. Books have been written to both attack and defend the practice of contemporary church. Some condemn any new innovation. Others go to extremes in church in the name of "reaching the unchurched."

Some boundaries are unavoidable and even obvious. You cannot believe in the Koran and still be a Christian, you can't affirm homosexuality or racism and be a biblical Christian, you can't not believe in the deity of Christ and be a Christian. There are definite boundaries in doctrine, but what about boundaries in practice? If my church has correct doctrine, can I do anything and everything to reach the lost? If "Lost People Matter to God" (a common slogan), can we do "Whatever it takes" (a common vision statement)? This attitude can be a positive development, but it also can also be twisted and abused.

Let me clarify one thing before we talk about boundaries of practice. I (Ed) am not "that guy." Neither is Dr. Towns. You know "that guy". He is usually a prominent pastor or theologian whose full-time ministry seems to be criticizing any new innovation. When I (Ed) was a seminary professor and afterwards visiting many colleges and seminaries, chapel speakers would visit and play the role of a self-appointed guardian of practice. Here is a partial list of what I have heard condemned in chapels: contemporary music, Hawaiian shirts, topical preaching, casual dress, pastors who don't hold their Bible, cultural relevance, praise choruses, songs (by name), and servant evangelism.

I have heard "that guy." I have listened to "that guy." I have rolled my eyes at "that guy." I KNOW THAT GUY!!! Please remember that I am not him—and neither is Dr. Towns. "That guy" is not to be confused with some wise leaders (both traditional and contemporary) who have asked some genuine questions about some recent innovations.

"That guy" makes it hard to have the discussion concerning the biblical boundaries for ministry today. To be fair, "that guy's" motivation is often not bad. Actually, his motivation is often the same as ours. He wants to preserve the faith, to keep it safe from compromise, and to hold up the Word of God unfettered by culture. "That guy's" motivations may be right but he has failed to escape his culture. It is ironic that he does the very thing that he condemns—allows his view of culture to overwhelm his ability to think biblically. He believes he is speaking prophetically against compromise. His attacks are intended to cause people to change. His agenda is that the "faith once delivered to the saints" (Jude 3) might always be upheld.

"That guy" feels strongly about it because he sees the precious Word of God, the faith, and the church as being soiled by new methods. He only knows the form (see earlier comments about form and meaning) and, to him, that form is being attacked and sullied. To him this is disrespectful, he sees great danger in compromise—after all, it WAS the liberal churches in the mid-1960s that tried to be "user–friendly," tried different methods of preaching, used new music, etc. He is unable to see that high content (being biblically sound) and high culture (being culturally relevant) are not mutually exclusive categories.

This is explained well in the Hughes scale that follows. Many Christians cannot distinguish between a biblically sound but culturally relevant church and one that is compromised by culture. For "that guy," any accommodation of culture is sin.

> The goal... is to be securely in Quadrant B—committed to cultural relevance and to biblical authority. Instead, churches tend to polarize around two axes of the scale. (Quadrant A churches are Bible focused but unable to relate to the lost world around it. Quadrant D churches can relate to the world but have abandoned the basic tenets of the faith.)... (T)he church that considers itself committed to biblical authority and opposed to cultural compromise (represented in Quadrant A), often is unable to understand a biblically faithful, culturally relevant missional church. Quadrant D churches are rightly

labeled as liberal—compromised by the world and co-opted by the culture. However, the Christian church is often unable to distinguish the Quadrant B (missional church) and Quadrant D churches (the trendy/faddish church). Furthermore, the quadrant A church is unable to see that contextualization is not necessarily the slippery slope to compromise. Lest we forget them, Quadrant C churches tend to focus on their traditions without any commitment to biblical fidelity.[1]

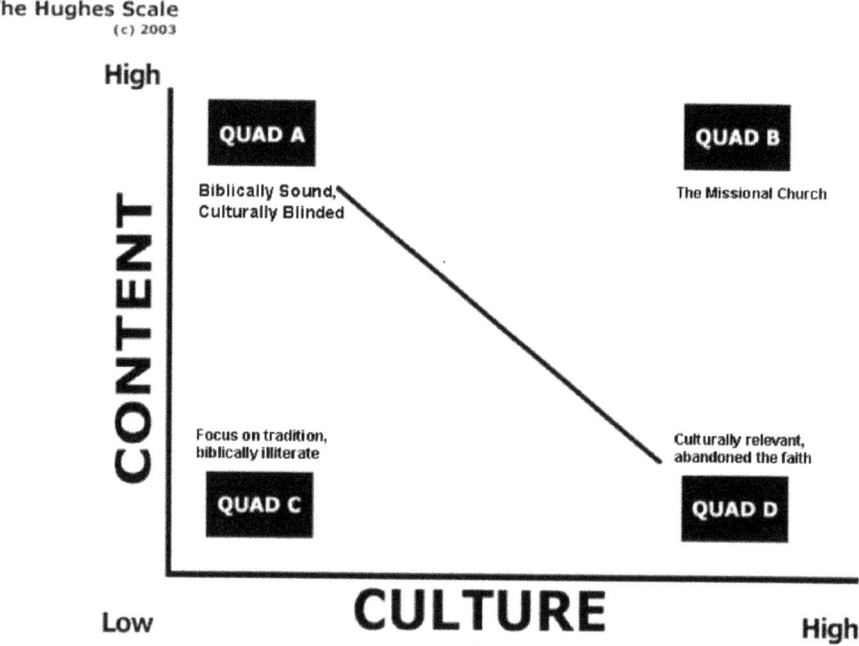

Why, then, do we need to address issues of practice? Practice is important. The Bible commands some practices and cautions others and condemns some. Everyone would agree that at some point, too far is too far.

When I (Ed) was a pastor, I knew that there were limits and some people went "too far." Of course, we thought that we never went "too far." (Would anyone knowingly go too far?) We believed we had "balance" and everyone else was too stiff, too wild, too contemporary, too traditional, etc.

---

1. Ed Stetzer, Planting New Churches in a Postmodern Age, (Nashville: Broadman and Holman, 2003), 16.

We thought we had found the perfect balance. Whenever I heard "that guy" preaching, I always discounted him and what he said.

As I look back, I realize that we were not so perfect. I realize that there were many places we did go too far and some that we did not go far enough. A real problem was that there was only "that guy" who was telling us we were going too far, and who wanted to listen to him?

After I left the pastoral ministry and became a professor, I (Ed) had a chance to visit many new churches. I came to two conclusions. First, "that guy" was not always wrong—there were churches that were doing the things he condemned. Second, there were a lot of good pastors and churches doing things because they "could," seemingly without thinking about their biblical significance.

Let me illustrate. A common practice in some new churches is to use popular film to illustrate the message. (Caveat #1: I have no problem with film.) One church I attended was using Scooby-Doo, a new film release at the time, to illustrate their message. (Caveat #2 I have no problem using film clips.). They sang a few songs—including the Scooby-Doo theme song, played a few quiz games, made a few jokes, then got into the message. (Caveat #3, 4, and 5: No problem with Scooby, quizzes, and jokes.) The message was a series of film clips followed by short explanations, a moral lesson from the film, and a Bible verse that (sometimes) related.

The church service troubled me—not because there was anything sinful about any of the elements of the service. (Remember all those caveats that show you I am not "that guy".) However, the church seemed to have no discernment about their objective. Their music did not glorify the Lord.[2] The preaching used the Bible for spiritual footnoting. We spent more time doing a "quiz show" than actually looking at a Bible verse. I began to observe that the lost world is becoming more and more spiritual while our churches are becoming less and less so in order to reach them. Would it not it be ironic if the world was more interested in discussing spiritual matters than the church?

Here's another example. A couple or years ago, I (Ed) visited one of the largest churches in the United States. It is well known—but don't try to guess, the church is not the point. The message that week was on "freedom."

---

2. (OK, I am tired of caveats, but I have no problem with any particular style of music—except Country Western, and everyone agrees with me, is of the devil.)

The speaker read a verse at the beginning, shared common-sense wisdom for 20 minutes though a series of three points (it was very good and inspirational) then shared a bible verse that validated the common sense.

The church taught Biblical principles but very little of the Bible. As a matter of fact the Bible verse at the beginning and the verse at the end had nothing to do with the 20 minutes of good common sense in the middle. (More on preaching later.) The point is this—why would I want to go to church just to hear inspirational secular music, a good drama, and 20 minutes of common sense squeezed between two short Bible readings?

I have no problem with… oh, forget it, you know by now. However, biblically based Christians need to carefully think through the repercussions of churches that teach biblical principles but not the Bible and that sing inspirational songs but do not teach people to sing to the Father. As one who has observed many churches in North America, we are doing more "doing" than "thinking."

If "That Guy" is a problem, he is not the only one. Let's talk about the "Other Guy!" There are pastors and churches that take things too far, they are the "Other Guy." They compromise in their attempts to be relevant.

Who is this "other guy?" In some ways it was me (Ed) at a younger age (more on that later). But, let me give a bigger picture. The "other guy" is often, but not always, young. In most cases, the "other guy" is deeply committed to the Lord and to reaching the lost. He (or she) is willing to cast off tradition and decorum if it will reach the lost. They are dissatisfied with the larger church and are looking for a better way. They are not intentional compromisers—quite the opposite, he or she is about taking the gospel seriously. They see a role model in Jesus—who defied tradition and condemned the traditional.

Here's the problem. "That guy" always has boundaries; "the other guy" has too few or none at all. However, both fail to satisfy. Both display biases and preferences that are not based on scripture. What we need to do is to look at practice with two assumptions:

1. Innovation is good because the unchanging gospel is reintroduced in a new culture.

2. Some innovation causes the gospel to be compromised.

There seems to be two kinds of innovation: those that are new expressions and are still biblical; and those that are new expressions that are not biblical. We must know the difference between them, but the problem is that like darkness and light, the perimeter is hard to locate.

This is certainly not as easy as the chapel speaker I heard condemn pastors wearing Hawaiian shirts. He said they were "pandering" to the culture (although he really had a pastor in Southern California in mind). "That guy" just preached against what he personally found inappropriate. All of us have preferences that express themselves as boundaries; this is how we feel in our 'gut': The chart below may help

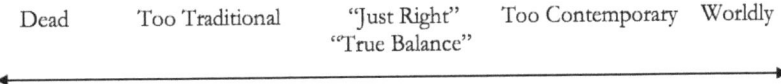

It can be hard to talk about boundaries because of "that guy." However, the fact that people are foolish **does not free us from the obligation to evaluate our own practices** in the light of scripture. We must not evaluate practices based on our own "gut" test. We need to evaluate them as either biblically inappropriate or as an indigenous communication of a biblical truth.

We all know what inappropriate is though we might not agree on what it looks like. Every church should desire to be a biblically faithful indigenous church. Why? Because we are now in a missionary setting in North America. Indigenous is a word from missions, but it is a key word that helps churches understand their ministry in the new mission field of North America today.

The word "indigenous" comes from farming. Plants are indigenous when they are native to an area. Or, in some cases, they become indigenous when they are planted and thrive in an area. For example, in the late 1800s, farmers brought oranges from Asia to California and later to Florida. Now, more oranges are grown in the Americas than in Asia.

Oranges have become indigenous to Florida and California. Oranges were once only indigenous in Asia… now they are indigenous to Florida and California. They are not indigenous to Northern Florida because it is too cold—they can't thrive there and thus will never be indigenous.

Missionaries Henry Venn and Rufus Anderson applied the "indigenous" concept to church life. They pioneered the concept in terms of the three-self movement—a truly indigenous church was self-supporting, self-governing, and self-propagating. Missionaries performed the task of transplanting the gospel into a new community, forming a new church with native people, and helping that new church establish itself in a relevant way to local culture, and therefore, become indigenous.

An indigenous church "fits" its community. If it is an African community, the church would have an African feel to it. We would not expect an African church to worship like an Anglo church—or even like an African-American church. Most missionaries have known this over the centuries, but tried to clearly define the terminology in 1938:

> An indigenous church, young or old, in the East or in the West, is a church which, rooted in obedience to Christ, spontaneously uses forms of thought and modes of action natural and familiar in its own environment. Such a church arises in response to Christ's own call. The younger churches will not be unmindful of the experiences and teachings which the older churches have recorded in their confessions and liturgy. But every younger church will seek further to bear witness to the same gospel with new tongues...[3]

Alan Tippett brought these ideas into more modern terminology in the 1960s:

> When the indigenous people of a community think of the Lord as their own, not a foreign Christ; when they do things as unto the Lord, meeting the cultural needs around them, worshipping in patterns they understand; when their congregations function in participation in a body which is structurally indigenous; then you have an indigenous church.[4]

Set Free Church (www.setfree.org) is indigenous as it ministers among Bikers—many who are former drug addicts and convicts. They have planted over 40 churches across the United States. The Overseas Chinese Mission Church (www.ocmchurch.org) in Manhattan tries to be an indigenous expression of the body of Christ in Chinatown. Reimagine (www.

---

3. International Missionary Council, "The Growing Church: The Madras Series," Papers Based Upon the Meeting of the International Missionary Council, at Tambaram, Madras, India, December 12-29, 1938. Vol. 2, (New York: International Missionary Council), 276, cited in Mark Terry, Ebbie Smith, and Justice Anderson, eds., Missiology (Nashville, TN: Broadman & Holman, 1998), 311.
4. Alan Tippett, Verdict Theology in Missionary Theory (South Pasadena, CA: William Carey Library, 1973), 136.

reimagine.org) is a missional community in San Francisco reaching people in an artistic and thoroughly postmodern community.

These churches all have different contexts. Yet, they proclaim the unchanging gospel of Jesus Christ in relevant but different ways in order to reach the people within their cultural setting. They are indigenous—they comprehend, and to some degree reflect, their cultural context.

In the end, a church can only be called "indigenous" when it reflects its cultural surroundings in such a way that it reaches that community. However, it should not become biblically unfaithful by becoming too similar to local culture. The indigenous church should be *contextualized* but not *compromised*.

To contextualize the gospel message is to walk down the top of a concrete barrier dividing two lanes of traffic on an interstate. If you jump whole heartedly into the past lane of tradition, you will be killed by obscurantism or dead form that means nothing to people today. If you jump completely into the modern fast lane of relevance, you will be run over by syncretism, pragmatism and compromise. It doesn't make any difference whether you're killed by culturally blinded drivers or culturally relevant drivers; to be dead . . . is dead. You must not compromise the uniqueness of Christ with history or syncretism.

Can indigenous be wrong? Of course. There are always certain actions or beliefs from a culture that do not need to be in church. Churches in mission fields struggle <u>every day</u> with this very issue. Should we be any different if we live in a mission field once again? Should we not struggle with scripture, culture, and practice like the rest of the mission fields? We think this struggle is best accomplished among friends (not "that guy" or "the other guy"), so let's dive in and talk about biblically-based indigenous churches.

In the coming chapters, we will address five common issues: church, worship, music, preaching, and evangelism. Our pattern will be simple. In each case, we will address what it will look like in a missions setting using our missionary story. Next, we will examine the boundaries—which are theological and which are cultural. We will conclude by giving examples of biblically faithful churches living and applying these truths in a culturally relevant manner.

QUESTIONS TO CHEW ON

1. Without identifying names, what types of people are "that guy" who insist on old out-dated practices and consider it a mark of biblical fidelity?

2. Have each in the group identify an "out-dated" practice that they still find meaningful. Why do others not use it? Why do some find it meaningful?

3. Have each in the group identify a new practice they think "waters down" Christianity. Why do some think the practice weakens Christianity? Why do some think it is effective?

4. What type of music is used in your church today that would have been considered inappropriate in the past? Why is it appropriate today? Why would it have been inappropriate in the past?

5. What do people wear to your church today that would have been inappropriate in the past? Why is it appropriate today? Why would it have been inappropriate in the past?

Chapter 4

THE HOLY SPIRIT IN NUMBERS

A Parable

The missionaries decided that the Nimo needed a church. They knew that a church was the Body of Christ and it extended His incarnation into a new setting. They knew that when they started the church, the converts who would come behind them would follow their pattern as THE biblical pattern.

So, they began to talk. "Well, what should we do to start a church?" asked the younger missionary. "Should we build a building?"

"Who needs a building?," the older missionary asked with a smile.

"What about hymnals?" the younger missionary asked.

"With what music," the older missionary asked with a growing grin. These are all questions we need to ask but we have to remember that what we decide will impact generations of Christians. We have to ask, What kind of music? What time? How long? What should worshippers wear? What should take place in church?

The only problem is that we should not give OUR answers, but we must give biblical answers that they can express in their culture. Yet, the Bible expresses no preference for worship time, length, and many other issues. So, let's just teach them the Bible and pray—and then ask the Holy Spirit to guide new converts to help us make these decisions."

What is a Church?

The Great Commission was given on five different occasions and, on each of these occasions, Jesus added more understanding to the Commission,, i.e., He added according to the increasing receptivity of His disciples.[1] When the Great Commission was recorded in Matthew, its target was more than the conversion of individual people. Jesus said, "Matheteusate panta te ethne" (Matt. 28:19). This is translated, "Make disciples of all the nations" (Matt. 28:19). The Church has the task of discipling the ethne, i.e., cultural groups or people groups.

From this command, we can make certain assumptions: First the word *ethne* implies we must get the Gospel into each ethnic group of people so that these people can become followers of Jesus Christ. Second, since discipling is an on-going challenge, we must get the message of Jesus Christ into the thinking, values, and life of each different ethnic group of people throughout the globe and throughout the ages. Third, effective evangelism implies winning people as a community and into a community, not just winning them as isolated individuals. Fourth, this challenge certainly includes evangelizing the post moderns cross-culturally for they represent a different ethne from previous generations. Once they are won to Christ, they are to be baptized according to a Trinitarian formula, and then taught everything that Jesus passed on to the disciples (Matt. 28:19-20). So what can be said about getting people into a local church?

1. The success of the Church does not depend on continuation of a modernity culture, but the creation of a New Testament church that reflects the new culture.

2. Because Jesus Christ is with us, ". . . I am with you always" (Matt. 28:20), we do not have to fear a new set of methods, or paradigms from postmodernity; but rather, we must focus on the power of Jesus Christ and His Gospel, which will be our new set of rules and paradigms.

3. Our challenge is not to continue our traditions or culture from modernity, or to create new customs for post moderns, but rather "immerse" every new believer into a community of like-faith believers from his or her culture, and

---

1. Towns, A Practical Encyclopedia, 97-98.

then give him or her the commission to reach others in that culture.

4. Being a disciple involves more than knowing the facts of Christianity, it also involves following Jesus Christ so that his or her Christianity is involved in experiences, relationships, learning, and serving.

5. To evangelize by making disciples is both a decision and a process. This means we must acknowledge that individuals are at different levels of understanding, feeling and readiness to respond to the Gospel. We must understand that following Jesus Christ is a decision when the person chooses to follow Jesus Christ, and then it becomes a process as the person continues to follow Jesus Christ.

6. The challenge is to evangelize every person in every culture so that he or she believes in Jesus Christ. Then, each one must "inculturate" Christ into his/her life and thinking, which involves making disciples within each ethnic group. We will not change the Church into the expectations of the postmodern, but aim to transform the postmoderns into the image of Jesus Christ. Many in a postmodern age may start farther away from Christ than their predecessors in a once nominally Christian America. It may take them longer to be assimilated into a culturally-Christian church in America, they can be assimilated more quickly into their ethnic church that has "acculturated" Jesus Christ.

The challenge of reaching post moderns for Christ is no different from past challenges of evangelizing un-reached tribes and nations with cultures different from the ones sending out missionaries or evangelists. The challenge of cross-cultural evangelism is the same while the conditions of the culture are new. Let's remember that God remains the same, His principles never change, and Jesus promises, "Lo, I am with you always, even to the end of the age" (Matt. 28:20).

To speak about church can be confusing. The church is a frequent topic of Scripture but many people fail to analyze what a church really is. Frequently, our perception of church is skewed by our cultural perceptions. Some see church as a large bureaucratic institution. For others, it is a building where people meet. Neither of these really describes the true definition of the church.

Jesus' first recorded mention of the church is in His dialogue with Peter: "I also say to you that you are Peter, and upon this rock I will build My church; and the gates of Hades shall not overpower it" (Matthew 16:18, NASB). Here Jesus described the foundation of the church on the faith of one of its first leaders.

In other places in the New Testament, "the word 'church' may be applied to a group of believers at any level, ranging from a very small group meeting in a private home all the way to the group of all true believers in the universal church."[2] The vast majority of biblical references refer to local churches (1 Thess. 1:1, the church of the Thessalonians; Rev 2:1, church at Ephesus, etc.).

The church is those who are "called out." The Bible uses the word ekklesia (in Greek) to say that the church would routinely meet together for purposes of worship, not just to be separate from the world.[3] A church meets and worships together.

One hundred years ago, missionaries were trying to determine what "made" a church a church. Most thought it would require buildings and prescribed rituals. One great missionary taught that the church did not require anything but what Scripture required. Roland Allen explained:

> ...[believers] were members one of another in virtue of their baptism. Each was united to every other Christian everywhere, by the closest of spiritual ties, communion in the one Spirit. Each was united to all by common rites, participation in the same sacraments. Each was united to all by common dangers and common hopes.[4]

---

2. Wayne Grudem, Systematic Theology: An Introduction to Biblical Doctrine (Grand Rapids: Zondervan Publishing House, 1994), 857.
3. Craig L. Blomberg, The New American Commentary vol. 22 Matthew (Nashville, TN: Broadman Press 1992), 253.
4. Roland Allen, Missionary Methods: St Paul or Ours? (Grand Rapids: Wm. B. Eerdmans Publishing Company, 1962), 126.

What then, is a technical definition of "church?" Is a group meeting in a home and studying the Bible a church? Should they partake of the ordinances and appoint biblical leaders? They may be a church—but they must <u>choose</u> to be a church. We will explain.

A church has been well defined:
> A New Testament church of the Lord Jesus Christ is… an autonomous local congregation of baptized believers, associated by covenant in the faith and fellowship of the gospel; observing the two ordinances of Christ, governed by His laws, exercising the gifts, rights, and privileges invested in them by His Word, and seeking to extend the gospel to the ends of the earth.[5]

A New Testament church is a group that sees itself as a church. A group can be a church when it sees itself as a church. It is "self-aware." Self-awareness alone does not make a church into a church. A house church of ten that sees itself as a church more closely fits the biblical description than a group of one thousand meeting on Tuesday night for Bible study. A New Testament church sees itself as one local church of baptized believers.

A church is "associated." It is not merely a group; it is a covenanted group. A century ago churches would post their covenants on the wall—showing all who visit their mutual commitments. This involved not only their moral resolutions, but also, their obligation to hold each other accountable to those resolutions.

The church also has practices and functions. Any true church rightly at least exercises the biblical ordinances of Baptism and the Lord's Supper. They are essential elements without which a true church cannot exist. These ordinances are only to be exercised by the local church. Believers who have covenanted with a local church also covenant to exercise spiritual gifts and to serve each other in a biblical fashion.

True churches present the Word of God. In the Bible this is called preaching. Some churches have tried to downplay the word "preaching." It is true that there is no secular use of the word that is positive—all are negative: "don't preach at me;" "he gave me a sermon." Some have called it "a message." Fine. However, the Bible does command us to "preach the word." The scriptures make it clear that preaching is essential:

---

5. "The Church," http://www.sbc.net/bfm/bfm2000.asp

"And as you go, preach, saying, 'The kingdom of heaven is at hand.' (Matthew 10:7, NASB).

And He said to them, "Go into all the world and preach the gospel to all creation. (Mark 16:15, NASB).

Teach and preach these principles (1 Timothy 6:2, NASB).

Preach the word; be ready in season and out of season; reprove, rebuke, exhort, with great patience and instruction. (2 Timothy 4:2, NASB).

If you prefer to translate that "message" rather than "preach," that is no problem. If you do not do it (preach) and do not do it with the prescribed tool (the Word), it is inappropriate. Biblical preaching is a mark of a true church.

The biblical offices are pastors and deacons. These offices are not included as cultural leftovers from the first century. The biblical offices are specific. God has called the church to have a pastor. He is to lead the church in a Christ-like manner as described in Scripture (1 Peter 5:1-4; Titus 1:5-9; 1 Timothy 3:1-7; Acts 6:2-4; Hebrews 13:17; Acts 20:28-31). Deacons are to serve the church by handling other matters to free the pastors for ministry. A church of every size is to have leaders functioning in such roles.

The Bible does not require that a pastor be ordained. It does not prescribe a certain course of education. It does require that he be a person of character who can lead and teach. The same biblical requirements are listed for deacons. They are to be selected by the congregation. In Acts 6:5, it was "the congregation that made the selection" of the deacons.[6] Paul appointed pastors in the New Testament. Most churches today endorse their own leaders. Even the "apostles and elders, not as independent bodies, not as one body separate from the church itself, [acted] in harmonious conjunction with the whole church."[7]

The planting and formation of churches must not be limited by man-made dictates. Man-made expectations have caused the church in North American to decline as the church around the world grows. While 50-80 million Christians meet in House Churches in China, many in North

---

6. John B. Polhill, Acts, New American Commentary Vol. 26, (Nashville: Broadman &Holman, 1992), 181.
7. Alexander, 88.

America are unsure if the group meeting in the apartment clubhouse can be trusted—since they have no church building.

As North American Christians, we must learn to affirm the kind of churches that scripture affirms. We must learn to "bless" and promote all forms of *scripturally sound* churches. These will include mega-churches, multihousing churches, rural churches, churches led by bi-vocational pastors, house churches, urban cell churches, and many others. If they meet the biblical standards, can we call them anything less that what God calls them? He calls them "church."

When is a church not a church?

There are certainly times when a church ceases to function as a church. They might claim the name church, but what takes place in their community disallows us to biblically affirm that truth. Churches are false churches when they intend not to be churches, when they defect from biblical truth, and when their practice removes the functions of a true church.

Some groups do not claim to be a church and should not be considered such. There are many good Bible studies and fellowships that do not claim the mantle "church." If they do not choose to adopt the characteristics of church listed above, they are not a church. Meeting together does not make one a church—meeting together with the intent of being a church does.

Some groups claiming to be a church are not because they have abandoned Biblical truth. Rev. Fred Nile, explaining his departure from the Australian Uniting Church (a liberal denomination that now ordains homosexuals), "They've adopted a policy which completely ignores the teaching in the word of God in the bible. I can't stay in a church which does that because in fact, to a degree, the Uniting Church ceases to be a church." He is right. When a church abandons the Bible, it cannot claim to be a true church. It has passed through the boundary of apostasy (more on that later).

Lastly, a church is no longer a true church when it abandons the functions of a church. Things like preaching, the Lord's Supper, Baptism, and other issues are not simply optional functions in a church. They are marks of the true church.

To Take Away

For many, this chapter is obvious. However, some are wondering if they are in a true church. They are wondering if their denomination is a biblical denomination. These are real issues that must be addressed. Some denominations have gone so far that they have adopted, as policy, doctrines that are contrary to scripture. The Uniting Church in Australia is such an example. In the United States, the equivalent is the United Church of Christ. Christians should not support such denominations. In Canada, the United Church has the same heretical doctrine. These churches have denied the gospel and are no longer true churches.

Yet, some churches have tolerated false teaching while allowing true teaching. This is difficult. Churches like the Episcopal, Presbyterian (PCUSA), and United Methodist churches have some individual churches (or even districts) that are false churches due to doctrine and practice. However, there are faithful Christians within those denominations where true churches battle with those that are false. These churches band together in groups called "Confessing Movements." In the Anglican Church, it is the churches outside of the U.S., British, and Canadian churches that are biblically faithful while a confession movement struggles within the "western" churches.

These Confessing Movements are "confessional." They hold to statements of faith (the "confessions") of their denomination. They are fighting against those who would change the doctrine and practice of the denomination. This seems like a lost cause to many. Yet in a recent Christianity Today article, "Turning the Mainline Around," tells a different story. Recent research has indicated that these confessional movements are working.[8] The Southern Baptist Convention ended its leftward drift. The United Methodists have made substantial progress. Difficult—yes. Impossible—no. These are churches that are in fellowship with false churches (always a dangerous place), but they are still true churches.

Some evangelical leaders and theologians met and produced a document entitled, "Be Steadfast: A Letter to Confessing Christians." In it, they pleaded:

> Much work has been begun by the various renewal movements among our churches. We note with thanksgiving the revival of Bible study, renewed interest in evangelization, fresh seasons of prayer, and renewed concern with the plight of the poor. We have committed ourselves to the ongoing life of the churches

---

8. Michael S. Hamilton http://www.christianitytoday.com/ct/2003/008/1.34.html

in which God has placed us, and we pledge our best efforts as theologians of the church to those who are engaged in this divine work of reform and renewal.[9]

QUESTIONS for Discussion:

1. When individual Nimo natives are won to Christ, each one has the light of Jesus in their life. When they come together, how much light must they generate before they become a local church? What must they do to become a church?

2. If false doctrine puts out the light of Jesus, how much false doctrine will God tolerate before a church stops being a church?

3. Can a group of Christians be a church if they have not called themselves a church, or if they have not "covenanted" to be a church?

4. What are some things found in the "nature" of a true church? What are some "forms" in your church that are not found in other churches that you consider a true church?

---

9. "Be Steadfast: A Letter to Confessing Christians," http://www.ird-renew.org/Issues/Issues.cfm?ID=487&c=9, no author, October 29, 2002. Representatives of two churches that were mentioned above, The United Church or Christ and the United Church, were included in this group. It will be controversial to include them as apostate churches. We only do so because they, in their governing documents, have adopted viewpoints that are anti-Biblical. These are not issues of interpretation, but of heresy. Obviously, not all will disagree, but it is discussion that needs to be had.

Chapter 5

WORSHIP

A Parable

The young missionary watched the Nimo converts worshipping God. They shouted as loud as they could when singing to God. It's the way they had worshipped their idols. They danced and jumped, violently shouting, "Glory to God" and "He is worthy".

The young missionary wanted the Nimo to worship as he did, with quiet reverential music. He told the older missionary that he would teach them to meditate on God as David did in the Psalms. The older missionary reminded his younger colleague that David danced before the Lord with all his might. The younger missionary frowned; the Nimo could have at least balanced some reverential music with some of their explosive music.

"Worship comes from the inner heart" the older man said, "A person must worship God with all their heart, soul and body." The younger friend argued, "The Nimo worshipped idols explosively, but it was false worship." He continued his reasoning, "The Heavenly Father is different from idols. The Father seeks His children to worship Him in spirit and in truth (John 4:24). The only valid worship is when the Father comes to receive it."

The older missionary said, "I believe the Father comes to receive the Nimo worship because they are serious."

"I don't", the younger missionary replied. "Sincerity is not enough. The Nimo must worship the Father in spirit and in truth. The worship of idols is completely different from the worship of the Heavenly Father."

The missionaries are making something difficult which is actually very simple. Worship is a face-to-face encounter with the Living God, based on a regeneration experience, prompted by the Holy Spirit, and results in the exhortation of God's glory. The word worship comes from the old English term "worthship." Simply speaking, worship is giving the worthship to God that He deserves because he is the Supreme Deity. Since worship is giving all of our praise to God with all of our hearts, then worship is an intense emotional, intellectual and volitional response to the majesty of God.

However, worship is also a growing entity within each believer. When people first become Christians, they worship with the intellect they have, but usually is very shallow. As they grow in their knowledge, experience and Christian service, then they give more to God in worship.

Worship is not optional to the believer, or is it simply a good discipline for a Christian to grow in grace. Worship is mandatory, because "the father is seeking (sincere worshipers) such to worship Him" (John 4:23). This passage goes on to describe that "they that worship Him must worship in spirit and in truth" (John 4:24). Look again at the Walla worship, if they know very little about God, they can only bring their past worship experiences into their present adoration of the Father. Is that acceptable? Unaccountable? However, when the Walla came to faith in Jesus Christ, they repented of their sins; which included repenting of the worship of false gods. Doesn't that mean they change both the object and expression of worship? At the very nature of God's Ten Commandments is the exhortation, "You shall have no other gods before Me" (Exod. 20:3). Also, God has commanded, "You shall not bow down to them (false gods), nor serve him" (Exod. 20:5). God goes on to say that He is a jealous God for any worship His people give to other gods or false gods. Therefore, the Walla should be careful not to confuse idol worship with worship of the Father.

Worship involves the intellectual process, but it is more than just the knowledge of God where people "worship Him in truth." Worship also stirs the emotions; but it is more than passion or sensual expression. Worship comes from a person's choice where they surrender their will to God, but it is more than a decision. True worship is moved by biblical facts to recreate the fundamental human experience of praise, adoration, and exultation of God. It is when the human cries out, "You are worthy . . ." (Rev. 4:11).

The measure of true worship is not about what worshippers do, because worship is measured by God's reception of the worshipper. If God does not come to receive a person's worship; then it is sterile. J. Oswald

Sanders has said, "In the act of worship, God communicates His presence to His people."[1]

As you travel from church to church, you will note that worship takes on many different faces. While the core of worship is centered on God, Christians worship in different ways. In some churches worship is reverencing God behind stained-glass windows while being surrounded by soft organ music, the worshiper's mind meditating upon the greatness of God. The next church may resemble a storefront revival meeting, interrupted with shouts of "Amen," or "Hallelujah," the service filled with electricity, excitement and energy. Some raise their hands while other drop to the floor, a few may dance, and some may even speak in tongues, while the focus is on worshipping God. Still, in another church, worship takes a completely different form. Behind clear glass windows, families sit together singing "Great is thy faithfulness," neither with emotional excitement nor meditative reverence. The focus of each worshipper is on God, where they give their tithes as worship to God, focus their thoughts on Bible-based sermons, and at the end of the service, pledge themselves to deeper love of God.

I (Elmer) have learned that my daily personal worship must be more than an activity; it must be an encounter with God. On some occasions I travel to a speaking engagement and become very weary; perhaps arriving late at night. Sometimes the next morning, my prayers seem to bounce off the ceiling and the words of scripture seem flat when I read them. That may be because I am weary or focused otherwise. Then I begin to worship God with the Lord's Prayer, praying: "Our Father who art in heaven, hallowed be Thy name . . . ." As I worship God through His many names, I find something happening in a drab motel room. The best way to explain what happens is through the movie in the late 80s, the Field of Dreams. The farmer in Iowa heard a voice saying, "If you build it, they will come," a reference to building a baseball field. I have applied that statement to my worship, "If you worship God, He will come." Since the Father seeks worship (John 4:23, 24), then when I worship Him he comes to receive my worship. That's when I experience the atmospheric presence of God. When I truly worship God, I feel His presence receiving my worship and it

---

1. J. Oswald Sanders as cited in Elmer Towns, Putting an End to Worship Wars (Nashville, TN: Broadman and Holman, 1997), 167.

becomes a "face-to-face" experience. I can turn a drab motel room into a sanctuary, i.e., the place where God dwells.

Perhaps one of the best books ever written on worship is Worship His Majesty by Jack Hayford. In this book Hayford indicates that worship is not just the adoration or praise that we give to God, "Worship is a two-way street." When we worship God, we get something in response, i.e., His presence gives us victory over sin, healing of emotions, power in Christian service, and a super-natural renewing of our love to God.[2] Ignatius of Antioch in defining worship said, "Come together to give thanks to God, and to show forth His praise. But when ye come frequently together in the same place, the powers of Satan are destroyed, and his 'fiery darts' urging to sin, fall back ineffectual. For your concord and harmonious faith prove his destruction, and the torment of his assassins."[3]

CHOICE IN WORSHIP

Historically, Protestants had two forms of worship, i.e., the *High Church*, and *Low Church*. The High Church was liturgical, reverent, and the worship service focused on God. High Churches were characterized by such activities as repeating the Apostle's Creed, corporately repeating the Lord's Prayer, responsive readings, singing the Doxology and Gloria Patri, beginning with an invocation to "invoke God's presence" and closing with a Benediction. The *High Church* has traditionally been found among Episcopalians, Lutherans, Presbyterians, and Methodists, even though they were originally Low Church in worship. In contrast, *Low Churches* were characterized as informal, simple, and congregational. In Low Church worship, you might have had activities such as: enthusiastic congregational singing, impromptu prayer, challenging sermons, and a feeling of community among Christians. The Low Church has traditionally been found among Baptists, Mennonites, Amish, Brethren, Pilgrims, Puritans and Anabaptists.

Historically, when Protestants moved, they always chose a new local church to join based on (1) denominations, (2) the church name, and (3) church doctrine. As an illustration, historically most Presbyterians never would have chosen a Pentecostal church or would have felt uncomfortable worshipping in lower churches. In the same sense,

---

2. Jack Hayford, Worship His Majesty (Dallas, TX: Word Publishers, 1987), n.p.
3. Towns, Worship Wars, 166.

Baptists have felt uncomfortable in the ritual Lutheran or Episcopal churches. This suggests that people have been comfortable in churches of their heritage, lifestyle, and values that were evident in churches where they grew up.

Most churches and denominations have passed their worship tradition on from generation to generation. However, lately churches or denominations have been influenced in the way they worship by interdenominational services (i.e., Promise Keepers), services on television, ministers trained in interdenominational seminaries, and various seminars on worship that are transdenominational. As a result, historic High Churches and Low Churches now are gravitating toward the same type of worship expression on a Sunday morning. Presbyterians who would have never attended a Pentecostal worship experience, now find that they are similar to many Pentecostal type worship experiences. As a result, it is easy for members of a High Church to sublimate their doctrinal or worship tradition, and worship or join a Pentecostal-type church when they move from one city to another.

This is an amazing shift. The worship of moderate charismatics has become the norm in many evangelical churches. People raise their hands, clap along with music, and sing not from books, but from screens projected overhead. These activities were avoided by most evangelicals twenty years ago, now they are so common they have become commonplace—they are the new traditional.

What is the primary source for this change? Is it coming from without the church, or from within? Culture seems to be influencing the church more than the church is influencing the culture in which the church is located. It's not one single factor that is influencing the church, but rather the whole thrust of society—the thrust of consumerism—is pushing the church into a different relationship with its worshippers/customers.

There is a powerful scene in a recent episode of the NBC show "Ed."[4] In this particular episode, Ed (and two others) visits the local church that is receiving some local headlines. There they see Rev. Porter and the worship of the "Heavenly Path Cathedral."

---

4. Episode Guide, Season 1, Episode 014, "Valentine's Day," accessed September 3, 2003; http://www.nbc.com/Ed/episode_guide/14.html.

When they enter the church, they hear a contemporary band playing upbeat music. Then, the music increases in tempo and they announce, David Lettermen style, "Ladies and gentlemen, put your hands together for..." Then we meet Rev. Porter as he enters to "high fives" from the band He begins his routine. He tells a joke to get started. He reads scripture in a voice imitating Jack Nicholson. Finally, he sits behind the desk and holds up humorous clips from newspapers. He calls this section, "headlines," much like Jay Leno. Ed and his friends leave the church before he gets to the message. But we can imagine what it would be like.

I (the author Ed, not the character!) am sure everyone laughed when the program aired. I didn't. I sat stunned—not because it was offensive—but because it almost seemed real. I have seen churches that are almost identical to this one. As I watched "Ed," I thought "I've seen churches doing that...and that...and that." I have seen pastor's do "headlines." I have seen pastors imitate movie characters. I have seen them be introduced in humorous ways. None of these in and of themselves are bad.

But, here is the irony—it was a joke. The producers were mocking the church—but in the process, they portrayed many of our attempts to "be relevant" and "contemporary." They illustrated the absurdity of many of our churches—and it hit close to home.

Most churches have no real basis for choosing what takes place in worship. Their only thoughts are, "will it attract people?" In other words, what will the consumer think?

Americans consume everything from clothes to entertainment to cars to furniture. As a matter of fact, consumerism drives the television industry, so without the commercial dollars, the average American could not be entertained by television as they would from four to five hours per day.

Advertising drives the entire business community of America. Why? Because consumerism is the engine that now drives the American society. Now the glue that holds America together is buying and selling. The service industry has become a dominant force, much larger than the manufacturing industry.

Less than 25 percent of our society is employed in manufacturing, and less than 5 percent of our society works on a farm. What does this mean? The majority of people work as salesmen, service technicians, consultants, managers, waiters; we sell to one another, service one another, and live off the profits of a consuming society. The new religion of consumerism has theologians that we call *advertisers*, and it has priests, that we call *salespeople*. The new religion has its temples that we call *malls*, and its worshippers are shoppers.

How has the consuming society influenced our churches? Notice the impact that culture has had on worshipping. People see church programs as menus, i.e., things to buy. The types of worship are the main entrees of the restaurant. In North America there are all types of restaurants with menus that fit the taste of various kinds of worshippers. Americans can select from fast food, Chinese, Mexican, fried chicken or a steakhouse. In the same way, they can go to a church that offers evangelism, Bible teaching, revival, psychological self-help, small group interaction, or mystical worship. This description of the current American church scene does not mean the authors approve of what they see. It's just the way it is.

Most American churches are no longer filled with doctrinal options, but with a variety of worship options. Americans go where they can feel comfortable with a particular style of worship, because it reflects their inclination and temperament. Most Americans never ask when they leave a church, "What did God get out of it," but rather they ask, "What did I get out of it." And if they get nothing out of the service, they don't come back to that service; they go where they get their worship appetites satisfied.

A Lutheran couple chooses a charismatic renewal church because they like the positive praise worship hymns. Perhaps they thought their former Lutheran church was dead. At the same time, a couple leaves their charismatic church because they feel singing the "bouncy" choruses through a projected PowerPoint presentation is superficial, so they leave and go to a Lutheran church because God is mystery, and they want to experience His reverential presence.

An Independent Baptist family leaves their evangelistic church service because they feel the sermon has become superficial with a gospel message over "John 3:16" Sunday after Sunday. They begin attending a Bible expositional church where they can learn the Word and meet God in scriptures. And yet, the opposite happens here; a couple leaves the Bible church because they're saturated (gorged) with Bible content, and they want an action-oriented service where people are getting saved and things are happening. They like "John 3:16" every SundayOne thing is evident in today's churches in America, there is a two-way door in and out of most worship services. People are entering to seek its strength, while others are tired of its routine and leave to seek their Sunday morning "fix" elsewhere.

So, the old phrase, "the church of your choice" no longer means a choice based on your history or your family, or even your parents. Like buying a t-shirt, or choosing a vacation destination, people choose a church based on what fits them best, what makes them feel comfortable and what satisfies them.

Most church leaders recognize six phases of worship styles in churches. These six worship styles are identified within the Protestant church: (1) the evangelistic church that focuses on winning the lost—in some cases by emphasizing evangelistic activity and preaching; in other cases through seeker focused services; (2) the Bible-expositional church that emphasizes teaching the Word of God; (3) the renewal church that focuses on expressing worship in contemporary worship choruses; (4) the body life church that focuses on fellowship (*Koinonia*) relationships and small groups; (5) the traditional liturgical church that focuses on reverential worship of God; and (6) the informal church of the common people, i.e., the church of the people, by the people, and for the people.

These six expressions of worship and/or ministries emerged on the American scene at the turn of the century. They are not mutually exclusive categories—there are some churches that overlap. At the center of each of these worship styles or "faces" are several catalysts (or types of glue) that hold these different churches together. Whereas, many Protestant churches will do many of the same things in worship or ministry—singing, praying, collecting money, preaching, and so forth—the way these things are done and the value that worshippers give to each of these, and the comfort level of the worshippers to each of these; make these six phases of worship different. Each ministry style adds an unique style to one's worship experience, making it different, and thereby, desirable.

Six Worship Styles

1. The evangelistic church
2. The Bible expositional church
3. The renewal church
4. The new life church
5. The liturgical church
6. The informal church of the people.

WHAT MAKES WORSHIP CHRISTIAN?

Worship is an experience, but just like conversion, all experiences are not Christian. Sincerity is not enough, even though we must worship God in "spirit." Also, correct knowledge is not enough, even though we must worship God in "truth." Worship is always a face-to-face relationship with God.

1. <u>Examination.</u> Christian worship begins when the worshipper examines his heart motions. Why am I approaching God? What do I want from God? What about myself, am I in right relationship to God? What is blocking my relationship to God? How can I remove barriers between me and God, how can I speak to God and He speak to me. What do I owe God? Worshippers needs to examine their own hearts; they need to see themselves as they really are. That means the worshipper must objectify his experience. We must see ourselves as we are, and we must understand what needs we have that only God can meet.

There are several worship experiences in the Bible; each one will help us understand what makes worship Christian.

<u>Isaiah in the temple (Isa. 6:1-13)</u>. When Isaiah saw the holiness of God in the Temple, he cried out, "Woe is me, for I am undone! Because I am a man of unclean lips" (Isa. 6:5). Note that before he could worship and connect to God, he had to honestly examine his own heart and realize the sin that hindered his relationship to God.

<u>Moses before the burning bush (Exod. 3:1-17)</u>. In the surroundings of nature on a mountain, Moses met God. In the burning bush, Moses saw the justice and purity of God and in that revelation of the holiness of God, Moses examined himself and cried out, "Who am I that I should go to Pharaoh" (Exod. 3:11). God commanded Moses to take off his shoes for the ground was holy. He was in the presence of God. It was then Moses saw his limitations and was ready to properly respond to God.

<u>Paul's experience on the Damascus Road (Acts 9:1-26)</u>. Even though this was an intense expression of emotions—perhaps Paul's conversion experience—it also contained elements of worship. Here was Paul zealously following his convictions (persecuting Christians) when suddenly he learns his whole perspective was wrong. Think of people who worship

God wrongly, even though they are as sincere as Paul was. In the Damascus Road experience, Paul met Jesus Christ. When he saw Jesus, he fell on his face and cried, "Who are you Lord?" (Acts 9:5). And next he cried out, "Lord, what do You want me to do?" (Acts 9:5-6).

To properly worship God you must properly examine yourself. When you see how far short you fall from God's holiness, then you must do something about it and prepare yourself for worship.

> 2. **Expectations.** When people come to worship God, they expect Him to show up. There is a certainly element of faith in true worship so that you believe God will meet with you, and in faith you make the right preparation, i.e., you cleanse yourself from sin and those barriers that prohibit a relationship with God.

The human spirit inevitably reaches out to God, and as you reach out to God in worship, you have faith that God responds and hears you.

Therefore, there must be an atmosphere of expectation that God will come to receive your worship. That atmosphere is pregnant with faith, i.e., that it is the leverage that brings the presence of God to you. The Psalmist cried out, "My soul, wait silently for God alone, for my expectation is from Him" (Ps. 62:5). So, in faith you must ask God to meet you; in faith, you must expect God to meet you, and in faith, you must prepare for your meeting with God.

> 3. **Appropriation.** Worship is a form of human activity. Just as a person can't go on a hike without walking, so a person can't meet God without worshipping. Therefore, they must appropriate the presence of God if they are to worship him.

You must appropriate what's offered in prayer, the scriptures, and from your knowledge of God; so you leverage the presence of God.

Worship is not overcoming the acquiescence of God, begging Him to come meet with you. No, "the Father seeks such to worship him" (John 4:23). The Father is available so, "If you worship Him, He will come."

> 4. **Meditation.** Some people worship God bombastically, singing great praise choruses, other people worship God

quietly and reverently, maybe in meditation or humming softly a quiet hymn. Some people sing loudly to block out the real struggle of life. They don't face their own limitations, nor do they face the holiness of God. Underneath, we all have deep and searching questions when the lights are out and nothing else disturbs our thoughts. We're all frustrated by our lack of ability to perform the demands upon us, or to fulfill our self-inflicted demands. We all grope for answers, seeking and searching for reality. And when it's quiet, we think about these things. Then we wonder about God. Where is He? What can He do for me? How can I approach Him? How can I get Him to help me?

In worship, these thoughts must be brought into focus; it is as we approach God that He tells us the answers to our questions, He shows us the solutions to our problems, and He establishes a relationship with us. So what does this mean? Meditation is not mere idle thoughts; meditation takes work, i.e., it takes work to worship properly.

Worship is not coming to the end of activity and effort, and just vegetating. Worship is not just quietness and reflection. Remember worship is a face-to-face relationship with God, it takes everything you've got to worship properly and effectively.

5. Consummation. Just as every mountain must have a peak, so every worship experience comes to a conclusion; but that conclusion is not just a Benediction or final prayer. The peak of your worship experience is your dedicated and changed life. You cannot enter the presence of God and go away unchanged. Just as the revelation of God demands your response, so the worship of God demands your conformity into His image. When your worship experience does not overhaul your thinking and transform your life, you need to ask yourself, "Did I really meet God?"

6. **Transformation.** Worship must do more than lead to dedication; it must also lead to transformation. Many people have dedicated their lives to God, but afterwards accomplished very little. When you dedicate everything to God, you come to the end of yourself, i.e., you surrender. Many nations have been beaten in war and surrendered. But as a beaten nation, they never rise like the Phoenix out of the ashes of their judgment to soar again. It's not enough to become "nothing," or to become a "worm in the sight of God." In worship, God transforms you into a useful instrument of service, or into a dedicated disciple, or into His image.

Remember, there is opposition to worship. When you worship, you will face a Satanic enemy, plus the lust of the flesh, and the temptations of the world are against you. You need a supernatural transformation to stand against your opposition. You have Divine enablement when you walk away from the presence of God. You have Divine power to leave the presence of God to go serve Him in a sin-driven world.

Why does worship transform? Because in worship you realize what you can't do, but you also see the greatness and strength of God. You cry out, "He is worthy, because in the worship experience you focus on the power of God and the person of the Lord Jesus Christ. When you kneel to God, He fills you with His presence; and it is through the power of Jesus Christ that you learn, "I can do all things" (Phil 4:13).

Moses worshipped God on the top of Mt. Sinai, it was there he experienced God's presence. When he walked again among his people, the people could not look upon his face for its brilliance. When the children of Israel saw the face of Moses, "the skin of Moses' face shown" (Exod. 34:35). Thus, when you truly meet God on the mountain, your life will shine when you walk again among the people of this earth.

CLOSING THOUGHTS

There are many new experiences of worship in contemporary America that we have apparently not seen before. Churches are taking advantage of film clips, PowerPoint presentations, praise bands, drama, narrations, and other forms of arts in their worship services. Some say these are good and necessary, for they reflect our rightful desire to reach people in emerging cultures, and the way they live is the way they will worship. However, many older Christians are not sure. They feel that these forms are not worship, "Because we have never done it that way before." Because the older folks can't worship using the cultural expressions today, they have rejected and/or condemned those expressions. They even question whether some of those expressions are true Christian worship.

A fire blazing in the jungle has its perimeters. The farther away you get from the fire, the less heat you feel in the cool night. Are the new expressions of worship pulling us away from the warmth of the fire or are they taking the fire to another location—as bright as before, but among different people? How far away from the fire do you have to become before you can't see to read, to walk safely, or to even live safely? Apply that to worship: is modern day worship moving Christians away from the light, i.e., towards cultural darkness? Because we are using instruments from culture, i.e., PowerPoint presentations, a praise band, clips from movies, and adapting the music of the world in our worship; are we moving farther from the light because we are identifying with cultural darkness, or are we bringing Jesus to them--sanctifying these tools and using them to expand the Kingdom?

QUESTIONS TO CHEW ON

1. American worship if we didn't attempt to reach the postmoderns with new methods, i.e., PowerPoint presentations, drama, contemporary worship music, etc.?

2. Are all six types of worship effective in today's world?

3. Since natives in the jungle don't have electronic aids in worship (PowerPoint presentations, synthesizers, electric guitars, etc.), what expressions of worship will best reach them?

4. What is the difference between the worship of a new and mature believer?

5. What are the "signs" that worship is losing its effectiveness among worshippers?

6. Since consumerism has influenced American worship, what would worship look like in a rural society, a pagan society, a Communistic society, or an Islamic society?

Chapter 6

MUSIC

The Parable

They could hear a loud noise in the distance. The missionaries were heading to meet with a gathering of Christians. Yelling and drums, some sort of horn... it was the Nimo way of making music. The missionaries started to hike that direction. As they got closer, they could make out a rhythm to the noise, and even some words. A few words were Christian words.

"That is some bad music," the younger missionary disliked what he heard.

"I am not a big fan myself!" explained the older.

The Nimo Christians were yelling Christian words with all their might. When they prepared for battle, or worshipped their idols, they shouted as loud as they could. So this was their natural reaction in singing for God.

"Hopefully we can teach them some good music," the younger missionary added. He wanted them to sing reverently, and thoughtfully.

The older missionary replied, "We need to teach them music that is "good" to them and good to God. I doubt they will like our piano music from America. But, if we can take our message and put it in their music, it will be good. It will be beautiful... not to my ear, but to God's. Ultimately, if God is glorified, that is good music. Good music will speak to their heart. We may not enjoy it, but the more important thing is that God is glorified."

"How do we know what is appropriate and what is not?" asked the younger missionary.

"That," the older missionary explained, "is a long journey...from total darkness to pure light." He went on to think about what he had just said and determined no matter what culture, most had to take that journey through the perimeter of light.

Fussing Over Music

Christians disagree about music style as much as other issue in the body of Christ. Each person has his or her own unique taste in music. To some, good music is always classical. To others, good music always has a country and western "twang." After all, if a person has a "country" or "Western" heart, shouldn't they worship God with the integrity of their heart? Still others enjoy music that may be described as rock or rap. If it's from their heart, shouldn't they sing that way? Still others like the swing music of the 40s, i.e., the "golden oldies." Can they worship God with soft melodies?

The fact is, Christians listen to, enjoy, and are edified by all of these kinds of music. But should they? A church introduced a worship band in its services. A church leader stood up in a meeting to declare, "I used to dance to the Devil's music before I was saved, I'm sure not going to attend a church that has a rock band, even if it's called a praise band."

Should the music of the church be entirely different in "sound" from the music of the world? Should there be a boundary between church music and worldly music? Some don't want their church to compromise in music, because the next step may be compromising their doctrine.

Let's examine the nature of music. In seeking to determine what is the right music for a church, it is important that we apply biblical principles to evaluate our music. That is not always easy—the Bible contains no music notes and God indicates no musical preferences.

Music is much like fire—morally neutral. Fire in the fireplace is good. Move it five feet over into the wall and fire is bad. How fire is used makes the difference. We need to understand there are some aspects of music that are neither immoral nor moral. Sometimes we *like* what we *like* just because we *like* it. The question is, "Are we using our new nature or our old nature to determine what we like about music in the church? Is there a middle ground in music? Is there an area where Christians have some liberty to choose what music to sing their praises to God?"

Three Types of Singing Taught in Scripture

There are only three types of singing explicitly taught in the scriptures. Paul mentions them to the Colossians, "Let the word of Christ dwell in you richly in all wisdom, teaching and admonishing one another in psalms and hymns and spiritual songs, singing with grace in your hearts to the Lord" (Col. 3:16). About the same time, Paul also wrote to the Ephesians telling them to be filled with the Holy Spirit and again listing the same three types of music they should be using, "Speaking to one another in psalms and hymns and spiritual songs, singing and making melody in your heart to the Lord" (Eph. 5:19). These three aspects of praise may be sung privately or in congregational singing.

> Three Types of Songs:
> 1. Psalms – Singing the words of scripture.
> 2. Hymns – Worship music sung to God.
> 3. Spiritual songs – Music to express our testimony.

The first aspect of church music is the singing of psalms. The book of Psalms has been described as the hymnbook of the Old Testament. A number of other portions of the scripture in both the Old and New Testaments may have been originally written as Psalms celebrating the greatness of our God. Throughout church history, Christians have sung the words of Scripture in a variety of ways. During the Middle Ages, much worship was limited to the Gregorian chants. Later, during the Reformation in Scotland, the singing of scripture was prominent from the Psalter. Today, scripture may be sung by a variety of praise choruses reflecting several different musical styles. In the last decade, a significant amount of music has been produced that is based on scripture and also contemporary in style—a welcome development to many.

The second aspect of church music identified by Paul is described as "hymns." Hymns, as we understand them, did not exist in the time of Paul's writing. He was not referring to a song such as "Holy, Holy, Holy." A hymn, by definition, was a song about, or to, God. Hymns cause us to reflect on specific aspects of God's character.

The third aspect of biblical music is described as "spiritual songs." These songs tend to celebrate our relationship with God and His mighty works, especially as they relate to our Christian life. These songs are important in helping us express our deepest experiences in the Christian life. They encourage both the singer and those who hear the song to continue enjoying their relationship with God.

Even though there are three aspects to scriptural music, not all three are used in every church service. Rather, different churches tend to emphasize one aspect of church music more than others. Scripture tends to be sung by the young or traditional reformed churches. Worship songs tend to be more often sung in liturgical churches. Praise or testimony music characterizes the singing one might expect in non-liturgical or contemporary churches.

These three types of music are explicitly commanded, meaning you must use them in your worship of God. Can it be suggested that if you do not use these three, are you are not obeying God? Notice what's missing. Paul didn't tell which type of music *not* to include.

While his commands are explicit to obey, can we implicitly use all other types of music to worship God? After all, if God didn't tell us not to use the native music that is indigenous to people's culture, couldn't a converted African use tribal drums to praise God? A converted Latino uses bongo drums to praise God? A new believer from inner-city Detroit uses the drum beat of hip-hop to praise God? Since God did not indicate a musical style, can any style be used to glorify God—if used appropriately?

Music has always been a struggle. It seems odd to hear Christians today insist that a certain style of music is best. Any Christian who reads history would know that there is no one right way. Take a look at the patterns throughout the centuries:

- *"Get rid of that flute at church. Trash that trumpet, too. What do you think we are, pagans?"*

- 200s A.D.: Instrumental music was almost universally shunned because of its association with debauchery and immorality. Lyre playing, for example, was associated with prostitution.[1]

- *"Hymns to God with rhythm and marching? How worldly can we get?"*

- 300s A.D.: Ambrose of Milan (339-397), an influential bishop often called the father of hymnody in the Western church, was the first to introduce community hymn-singing in the church.[2] These hymns were composed in metrical stanzas, quite unlike biblical poetry.

---

1. Andrew Wilson-Dickson, Story of Christian Music (Minneapolis: Fortress, 1996), 28.
2. Eerdmans' Handbook to the History of Christianity (Grand Rapids: Eerdmans, 1977), 140.

- They did not rhyme but they were sometimes sung while marching.³ Many of these hymns took songs written by heretics, using the same meter but rewriting the words.⁴
- *"The congregation sings too much. Soon the cantor will be out of a job!"*
- 500s A.D.: Congregations often sang psalms in a way that "everyone responds." This probably involved the traditional Jewish practice of cantor and congregation singing alternate verses.⁵
- *"Musical solos by ordinary people? I come to worship God, not man!"*
- 600s A.D.: The monasteries, referencing "Seven times a day I praise you" (Ps. 119:164), developed a seven-times-daily order of prayer. The services varied in content, but included a certain amount of singing, mainly by a solo singer, with the congregation repeating a refrain at intervals.⁶ The services were linked together by their common basis in the biblical psalms in such a way that the whole cycle of 150 psalms was sung every week.⁷
- *"Boring, you say? Someday the whole world will be listening to monks sing these chants."*
- 800s A.D.: Almost all singing was done in chant, based on scales that used only the white keys on today's piano. The monastery was the setting above all others where Christian music was sustained and developed through the Dark Ages.⁸

---

3. Wilson-Dickson, Story of Christian Music, 36. See also Harry Eskew and Hugh McElrath, Sing with Understanding (Nashville: Broadman/Church Street Press, 1995), 86-87.
4. Steve Miller, The Contemporary Christian Music Debate (Wheaton: Tyndale, 1993), 109.
5. Wilson-Dickson, Story of Christian Music, 30.
6. Eerdmans' Handbook, 216.
7. Wilson-Dickson, Story of Christian Music, 33. See also Donald Hustad, Jubilee II, second edition (Carol Stream, IL: Hope Publishing Company, 1993).
8. Wilson-Dickson, Story of Christian Music, 34.

- *"How arrogant for musicians to think their new songs are better than what we've sung for generations."*
- 900s A.D.: Music began to be widely notated for the first time, enabling choirs to sing from music. Thus new types of music could be created which would have been quite out of the reach of traditions where music was passed on by ear.
- *"Hymns that use rhyme and accent? Surely worship should sound different than a schoolyard ditty!"*
- 1100s A.D.: The perfection of new forms of Latin verse using rhyme and accent led to new mystical meditations on the joys of heaven, the vanity of life, and the suffering of Christ.[9]
- *"This complicated, chaotic confusion is ruining the church!"*
- 1200s A.D.: Starting in France, musicians began to discover the idea of harmony. The startling effect of the choir suddenly changing from the lone and sinuous melody of the chant to two-, three-, or even four-part music did not please everyone. One critic commented how harmony "sullies" worship by introducing a "lewdness" into church.[10]
- *"Don't try to sing that hymn at home; leave it to the professionals at church."*
- 1300s A.D.: Worship in the great Gothic-era cathedrals and abbeys used choirs of paid professionals, "a church within a church," sealed off by screens from the greater building. Ordinary people generally had no place in the

---

9. Harry Eskew and Hugh T. McElrath, Sing with Understanding (Nashville, TN: Baptist Sunday School Board, 1980), 91-92.
10. Andrew Wilson-Dickson, Story of Christian Music (Minneapolis, MN: Fortress Press, 2003), 52.

spiritual life of these great buildings, except perhaps in the giving of their finances.[11]

- *"It's too loud, and the music drowns out the words."*
- 1400s A.D.: Music became increasingly complex (Gothic sounds for Gothic buildings), prompting criticisms that only the choir was allowed to sing. As reformer John Wycliffe had complained, "No one can hear the words, and all the others are dumb and watch them like fools."[12]
- *"They want us to sing in today's language. Shouldn't God-talk be more special than that?"*
- 1500s A.D.: The new prayerbook, pushed by King Henry VIII of England decreed that all services would be in English, with only one syllable to each note."[13]
- *"Now they're putting spiritual words to theater songs that everyone knows."*
- 1500s A.D.: Martin Luther set about reforming public worship by freeing the mass from what he believed to be rigid forms. One way he did this was by putting stress on congregational singing.[14] "Although Luther led the revolt against the abuses of the Roman Catholic church, he continued to make use of its texts and tunes. He modified Roman Catholic tunes and texts to fit his new theology. As a result, people recognized familiar hymns and chants and felt at home in the new church. He used music which was already familiar to the majority of the people in Germany."[15] As one writer quipped: "The Catholic, in church, listens without singing; the Calvin-

---

11. Ibid., 46.
12. Ibid., 56.
13. Barry Rose in Heavenly Voices, Gateway Films/Vision, 1998, video.
14. Eerdmans' Handbook, 363.
15. Eskew and McElrath, Sing with Understanding, 99.

ist sings without listening; the Lutheran both listens and sings–simultaneously!"[16]

- *"Okay, men on verse 2, ladies on verse 3, and the organ on verse 4."*

- 1600s A.D.: The organ played an important part in Lutheranism, Anglicanism, and Roman Catholicism, while in the Reformed churches there was much opposition to it.[17] Initially the organ was not used to accompany congregational singing, but had its own voice, often substituting for a sung part of the service. As a result, the organist would often play a verse on the congregation's behalf.[18]

- *"Our children will grow up confused, not respecting the Bible as an inspired book."*

- 1700s A.D.: Isaac Watts gave a great boost to the controversial idea of a congregation singing "man-made" hymns, which he created by freely paraphrasing Scripture. Charles Wesley paraphrased the Prayer Book, and versified Christian doctrine and experience. Wesley's songs "had at least as great an effect as his sermons."[19]

- *"Their leader is just asking for trouble when he says, 'Why should the devil have all the best music?'"*

- 1800s A.D.: William Booth, founder of The Salvation Army, used rousing melodies with a martial flavor to set the tone for his Army. He is credited with popularizing the "why should the devil" question cited above.[20]

---

16. Wilson-Dickson, Story of Christian Music, 81
17. J. D. Douglas, Walter Elwell and Peter Toon, Concise Dictionary of Christian Tradition (Grand Rapids: Zondervan, 1989), 259.
18. Wilson-Dickson, Story of Christian Music, 76.
19. Eerdmans' Handbook, 426-427, 448.
20. Wilson-Dickson, Story of Christian Music, 139. Some sources attribute the concept to Martin Luther. See Richard Friedenthal Luther, His Life and Times, trans. by John Nowell (New York: Harcourt Brace, 1967), 464.

- *"These Christian radio quartets are on a slippery slope. Don't they realize that the airwaves are the domain of Satan, 'prince of the power of the air'?"* (Eph. 2:2).
- 1900s A.D.: When radio was in its infancy, a handful of Christian pioneers such as Donald Grey Barnhouse and Charles E. Fuller began featuring gospel music and evangelistic teaching over the airwaves. Many Christians initially showed skepticism.[21]
- *"Christian Rock is an oxymoron. The music of the world must not invade the church."*
- 1970s A.D.: Larry Norman sang, "I want the people to know, That He saved my soul, But I still like to listen to the radio…They say that rock and roll is wrong…I know what's right, I know what's wrong and I don't confuse it: Why should the devil have all the good music…'Cause Jesus is the Rock and He rolled my blues away." He founded what became known as Contemporary Christian Music… and it is still controversial today.[22]

Four Things That Make a Song

Before we can evaluate music, it is important to recognize that there are four different parts to a song. These are not Biblical descriptions, but they are technical descriptions that will help us to discern the purpose and impact of a song. (Not all cultures will have all of these parts, but the vast majority do.)

The first of these parts is the *melody*. Most music begins with a melody, which is the theme or signature of the song. Melody refers to the dominant series of notes running through the song that makes it a unified whole. Melody is usually tied to the words of a song and helps communicate its meaning. While melody stirs the heart, the words speak to the mind.

---

21. Special thanks for the ingenuity of Warren Bird in presenting this material in book co-authored with Elmer Towns: Into the Future: Turning Today's Church Trends into Tomorrow's Opportunities (Grand Rapids, MI: Fleming H. Revell, 2000), 139.
22. Ibid.

The second part of most music is *harmony*. Harmony is simultaneous combination of tones, chorded structures as distinguished from melody and rhythm. Our emotions are stirred by harmony. When harmony is written in major chords, the song helps us feel positive, or joyful, or victorious. When harmony is written in minor chords, the music reflects our lower, somber or negative feelings.

The third part of music is *rhythm*, which is the beat. Every song has some rhythm, which is the timing that is measured by a metronome. In some musical styles, rhythm is more dominant than in other styles, such as rap, which is almost exclusively rhythm. Rhythm tends to affect us physically. Military music makes us want to march, while some worldly rap—supported by anti-God words—stir our lust and lower nature. And all county western music is of the Devil. (OK, not really, just a joke from Ed.)

The fourth part of a song is the *words*. Usually, the words and melody reinforce one another. The words of a song are the heart of the song. Words carry the message that is communicated by the music. When melody, harmony and rhythm are related to the words, the song speaks to us. The music we enjoy most is that which is closest to our personally preference, or it expresses our values or attitude.

When asked, "What makes a good song?" my (Elmer) friend David Randlett[23] uses a chicken as an illustration. In his illustration, the meat of the chicken is the melody, the barbecue sauce is harmony, and the salt is the rhythm. When you barbecue a chicken, the proper blend of chicken, sauce and salt is the key. Good taste is the key to determine if it is good music.

How to Test Your Music

We all have different preferences when it comes to the way we like our meat cooked. The same is true in the area of music. We must test everything by the Word of God. All of us are responsible to interpret the Bible and apply it to our life but this is where disagreement comes because we interpret differently. Music is a form that is used to convey meaning. It may be the most challenging of all forms because it involves preference, emotions, vocalization, etc.

The following seven test statements each relate to biblical principles that we should apply to our music to determine if it is Christian. Examine these seven test statements to determine if the music you prefer is Christian.

---

23. Dr. David Randlett a professor of music at Liberty University in Lynchburg, Virginia.

The first test is the *message* test. This test examines the words of the song to consider its message. Does this song express the Word of God? Does the message lift us, i.e., appeal to our higher nature, or do the words appeal to our lower nature? If we seek to glorify God, it is important that the message of the songs be consistent with the known and revealed will of God.

The second test to apply to our music is the *purpose* test. All music was written with a purpose in mind or heart. Determine whether the music is sad, joyful, uplifting or soothing. And again some music is designed to tempt you to sin, because it stirs your lust. Some "protest songs" of the "Hippies" were designed to get you to rebel against your government. Music that may be appropriate at one time, may not be appropriate at another time. When we apply the purpose test to our music, we choose songs that reflect our emotions or are likely to produce the emotion we wish to feel.

Third, we need to apply the *association* test. No music exists in a vacuum. The association test asks the question, "Does the song unnecessarily identify with things, actions, or people that are contrary to Christianity?" An otherwise good song may be rejected because of its associations with ungodly people, or worldliness, etc.

The churches that I (Ed) have pastored have generally used contemporary music. I remember coming into the worship team's rehearsal. They were rehearsing "Amazing Grace." This was not a song we sang frequently—and they were putting it to a new tune. That was the problem. Nothing was wrong with the song. However, the tune they chose was from another song: "The Rising Sun" or "There is a House in New Orleans." Various artists have recorded it. If you know the tune, you will see that it fits nicely.

I explained to them that the association of the song would be unavoidable—the original song would impact the meaning today. The original song was from the drug culture.

I (Ed) was reminded of this when speaking to a group of pastors, some of whom were Jamaican. I was challenging them to consider that there is no such thing as Christian music, only Christian lyrics. I asked if God could use jazz; they said yes. I asked if God could use country/western, they said yes. I asked a few others; then I asked if God could use reggae. They were shocked and clearly expressed that it was not appropriate. Reggae music was about drugs and there would be no reason to sing about drugs in church. They had a point.

I then asked if it would be OK to use reggae music in my church where we have no concept of the drug connection. They agreed. The music was not the problem, the association was. The key question for the association test is this, "What does the music bring to mind in the heart of the worshipper?" Note, not what does it inspire in my heart—but what does it inspire in the heart of the worshipper.

For example, for me and for many others, rap music is about violence and misogyny (women hating). However, to some, it is about raging against *something*. Therefore, if the worshipper finds that the music helps him or her to rage against sin and the world, such a music can be associated with angst and struggle, but against something that matters. For example, one group sings:

> Man is nothing, but you think that you're bad
> Fool if it wasn't for my God, I would have already had you
> Deny His name are you willing to admit it
> And if so, are you willing to die for it
> Cuz I am, He is my life and I don't fear death
> Cuz he already paid the Price

What P.O.D. has done in their song "Preach" is to take a form and to use it for a different meaning. The form of rap is no less godly that the form of 4/4 time in most of our hymns. It is a canvas waiting for a picture. It does convey and associate—angst against something. P.O.D. has followed the pattern mentioned earlier:

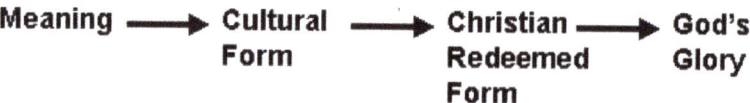

The fourth test is the *memory* test. We tend to associate our memories and experiences with significant songs in our past. This can be positive or negative. The memory test asks, "Does the music bring back things in your past that you have left?" Remember, repentance is a significant step in conversion. If you have left the darkness, don't sing those songs that make you want to return to the darkness. A song that may be enjoyed by some Christians should not be used by others who struggle with past memories.

This does not mean that we need to abuse the notion of "offending our brother." It seems that many churches have adopted a "don't-offend-anyone policy." That is not what the scripture teaches. Scripture teaches that if what we do causes people to sin, we ought not to undertake a particular practice. Listening to contemporary music does not cause the senior adult to *sin* though it does offend—there is a distinct difference. The association test says, "Don't use music that will lead people to sin." It does not say, "Don't use music that some will find distasteful."

The next test is the *emotions* test. Music stirs our emotions. Both negative and positive emotions can be stirred by music. The emotions test asks, "Does the music stir our negative or lustful feelings?" Christian music should stir our passion for godliness, prayer and righteous living. If music stirs your lust and makes you idolize or crave sin, it is wrong; no matter how innocent it may appear. This test causes us to evaluate how music affects us emotionally.

The *understanding test* seeks to determine the meaning of the song. Should we use music that we don't understand or have a difficult time finding the melody? Some people enjoy and understand classical music. Other people can't tolerate it or hate it. Others enjoy and understand country/western. Again, other people can't tolerate it or hate it. Applying the understanding test, those who appreciate classical music would find it easier to worship God listening to a recording of Handel's *Messiah* than a southern gospel quartet.

The final test may be described as the *music* test. This, like many of the others, is a "cultural" test that will differ from place to place. It asks, is there a "song within the song?" The music test looks at the song to determine its merits based on hymnology. It seeks to determine if the song is singable, if it flows comfortable from one line to another. Does it make your heart join in the song? A song may have Christian words and is sung by a dedicated follower of Jesus Christ, but the music is flat and leaves the audience empty. That particular song will probably pass out of existence because it fails the *music* test.

The history of church music suggests that every generation has its own music. Today, many older Christians reject the contemporary music of the younger believers, while the younger don't understand or use the music of past generations.

These tests lead us to one simple conclusion: God can use **ANY** form of music. God has no musical style or preference. Therefore, with the exception of the message and purpose test, the only tests that we have provided are cultural. The question is asked, "What impact does this music have on the culture via association, memory, emotions, understanding, and music?" These are not easy questions—but they are essential.

When a worship team is choosing music, it needs to think through some important issues. They may have the freedom to choose, but discernment calls them to choose wisely.

The use of secular music in churches is an important issue today. Some churches choose to use secular music to put the audience at ease. However, most secular songs will not pass the tests listed above. Yet, any musical style can pass the test in the right context.

Music across the Perimeter

There is a perimeter between light and darkness. So there is a difference between the music of God and the music of the world. The problem is the twilight zone. There is not a "hard" boundary line in church music, but a gray perimeter between light and darkness.

For many, it is easy to define the boundary. They can just "feel" it. If music does not minister to them, it must not be used in church. If it offends their style, it must be Satanic. They think God could never use such music. The only problem is that the music you enjoy was probably considered unspiritual when it first came onto the scene. So, we need more than a preference test, we need a discerning way to evaluate music.

Christianity is a *rational* religion, so we must use our minds to determine how to best glorify God through music. Christianity is also heart, so we must examine our attitudes and values to determine what music is doing to us. Different music leads people in different ways to different places, so there is a twilight zone where it is difficult to determine if we are standing in light or darkness.

Finally, Christianity is choice, involving the whole person. So our faith must always confront our intellect, emotion, and will. We can easily see bright light and see absolute darkness. As we stand in the gray twilight zone, we must determine where we let our music take us.

QUESTIONS TO CHEW ON

1. Have several suggest a Christian song that used to be meaningful to them, but has lost its meaning. Why?

2. Why does most Christian music usually last only two or three generations? Suggest some Christian music that is several generations old.

3. Is there any Christian music or song that has endured since the early church? Why not?

4. Have several suggest a contemporary Christian song they like. Have them give reasons why they like it.

5. Have several suggest what Christian music has touched their heart the most and drawn them closer to God. Why?

Chapter 7

PREACHING

The Parable

The younger missionary had preached to the Nimo Christians a sermon on building a Christian family, but the sermon hadn't gone over well. The concept of the family unit was entirely different to their concept of the tribal unit. Yes, the Nimo paired up in male-female relationships, but they lived as a tribe. Everyone worked together and ate together. The younger missionary never established a point of contact.

The older missionary wanted a Christian Nimo to preach to the Nimo in their own heart language. So a Nimo tribesman who had been taught to read scripture was brought forward to "share" the gospel with the new believers. But as he began to speak, his presentation was absolutely different than anything the missionaries had ever heard.

The Nimo Christians chanted Revelation 4:1, "After these things I looked, and behold, a door standing open in heaven." He repeated the scriptures three times with a sing-song delivery, then the others repeated the identical words and rhythm.

The Nimo Christians then chanted the next phrase, "And the first voice which I heard was like a trumpet…saying, 'Come up here'" (Rev. 4:1). After the believers repeated the identical phrase, the leader went back to repeat the first phrase. The Christians followed.

For the next 45 minutes, the Nimo leader chanted his way through Revelation 4, the new believers repeating every phrase over and over again. The Nimo leader had given a picture of heaven. When he came to the end of the chapter, he cried out "worthy." They all began to shout at the top of their voices, "worthy."

The young missionary was glad the new Christians mimicked a whole chapter of scripture, but it was not a sermon. At least, the kind of sermon he was used to hearing. He whispered to the older missionary, "The leader didn't explain the Bible."

The older missionary answered, "The Holy Spirit can do that."

I (Elmer) witnessed a group of new believers in the mountains of Haiti doing exactly what we just described. The sermon for the evening was Revelation 4; they heard what heaven was going to be like. Because they were a tribe, they bonded together by repeating together and to show their emotions, they got louder.

Everybody seems to be an expert on preaching because everyone who listens to a sermon has an idea whether they like it or not; whether it's good or bad in their opinion. False boundaries abound when it comes to preaching. Many from conservative theological sources say that the only true form of preaching is one that is not found in the bible—verse by verse exposition. Others think that anytime someone talks about biblical principles, that is the same as preaching the Bible.

Many think that the only valid form of preaching is verse-by-verse. To some, expository preaching seems to be a word by word analysis of a text in linear and sequential manner. To others, it seems that one is expository as long as one uses a long enough passage and then dissects it for the points. To still others, expository preaching simply requires a main text from which to work.

John R. Stott defines it better—an expository sermon is simply a sermon with the biblical truth as its basis. (Stott corrects the notion that the only true preaching is the form of exposition he calls "running commentary.")[1] Regardless, when verse-by-verse preaching is presented as the only form of valid preaching, it is a false boundary from church culture.

Boundaries of Preaching

Biblical preaching, if not verse-by-verse preaching, must include something to make it a biblical "message" rather than a "speech." The Bible does say to "preach the Word" (2 Tim. 4:2). New methods of preaching have emerged, but they still must be evaluated in light of this biblical command.

---

1. 1 John R. Stott, Between Two Worlds: The Art of Preaching in the Twentieth Century (Grand Rapids, MI: William B. Eerdmans Publishing Company, 1982), 125.

To some in evangelicalism today, anything but verse-by-verse expository preaching will not "interpret, understand, explain, or apply God's truth."[2] However, we think this is a false boundary. Since there are no biblical or historical references to such preaching in the early church, it is hard to make the case that it is the only form of preaching.

Possible examples of verse-by-verse teaching can be seen in the Bible. The first (and clearest) example is in Nehemiah. The Levites "read from the Book of the Law of God, making it clear and giving the meaning so that the people could understand what was being read" (Neh. 8:8, NKJV). In this passage we find reading the scripture, explaining and making clear the text, an understanding of the message. If expository preaching is anywhere in the Bible, this is it.

The second example is less clear. Here in the New Testament Jesus explains all the scriptures about himself.

> *"And beginning at Moses and all the Prophets, He expounded to them in all the Scriptures the things concerning Himself"* (Luke 24:27, NKJV).

It is unlikely that Jesus did a grammar study of Isaiah 53. If so, did he also exegete Micah and the Psalms? It is significantly more likely that Jesus used specific texts to show that he was the Messiah.

So, the idea of verse-by-verse preaching is a cultural boundary, rather than a biblical one. If it is God's plan for us to use verse-by-verse preaching, why is it not recorded in the scriptures? If the first true expositor was John Chrysostom[3], then how can we hold up the standard of verse-by-verse preaching as the biblical model? It was Origen who first began to apply the principles of classical scholarship to preaching.[4] Thus, how can we consider word studies and grammar studies to be the biblical mandate?

When looking at boundaries, we have to determine what is NOT commanded but acceptable (verse-by-verse preaching) and what is essential (biblical preaching). Verse-by-verse preaching or not, the command of scripture is clear:

---

2. Richard L. Mayhue, "Rediscovering Expository Preaching" in Rediscovering Expository Preaching, Richard L. Mayhue, ed. (Dallas: Word Publishing, 1992), 9.
3. Ibid., 44.
4. Edmund P. Clowney, "The Purpose of Preaching" in Leadership Handbooks of Practical Theology, Vol. 1: Word and Worship, James D. Berkley, general editor (Grand Rapids, MI: Baker Book House, 1992), 15.

"Preach the word! Be ready in season and out of season. Convince, rebuke, exhort, with all longsuffering and teaching. For the time will come when they will not endure sound doctrine, but according to their own desires, because they have itching ears, they will heap up for themselves teachers" (2 Tim. 4:2-3, NKJV).

If the word is preached and it accomplishes the biblical objectives—"correct, rebuke and encourage"—then we have "preached the word." If that sermon takes a verse-by-verse form, then it accomplishes that biblical objective. If not, that is acceptable as well. As long as the scripture sets the agenda of the text and the scripture is faithfully delivered.

On the one extreme is the insistence of verse-by-verse preaching. On the other extreme is the church that preaches biblical principles and not the Bible itself. I (Ed) recently attended a well-known church that was leading a series called, "(church name) at the Movies"

It was not an unusual service—it is very similar to a lot of the other "edgy" churches out there. A clip from Mel Gibson's "Braveheart" started the service. (It was part two of the series that included several other popular films.) The service was built around six lengthy video clips from the movie.

The service was done well. They even had a professional bagpiper come through to focus on the Scottish theme. What they were trying to do made sense. They were searching for cultural points of contact to teach biblical truths. They did that—but they did not "preach the word."

The speaker was transparent. He explained that the church had chosen these movies to find themes. They did so in a survey. This week the main theme was, "What do I need to be to be a William Wallace-like character?" There was a lot of good to emulate. The speaker explained that he would "try to shrink a three-hour movie into three categories." All throughout the message, the picture of William Wallace (aka Mel Gibson) with a sword, fire, and blood was on the screen.

One point explained, "It is our wits that make us men." The speaker emphasized the importance of not seeking revenge. After showing the clip, explaining the context, and telling the story, the speaker indicated that we should "run from revenge." Then, he brought in his first scripture reference. He explained, "This is consistent to what William Wallace might have heard taught in Matthew 26…"

None of this was bad. It was not liberal. It was not compromise. They preached biblical principles. They used cultural examples to prove the validity of the scripture. Using cultural icons to introduce the Christian message is a time-honored evangelistic strategy, but it does not meet the "preach the word" standard.

Connecting with culture is good, and using contemporary examples can be powerful. However, the Bible must take the center of any true preaching. It should involve the "exposing" of God's Word.

Expository Preaching That Is Biblical

In the church service discussed above, the pastor used the Bible to illustrate his sermon on "Braveheart" (rather than the other way around). That does not constitute biblical expository preaching. Expository simply means a presentation of the meaning or intent—in this case, of a particular biblical text. True biblical preaching should always be expositional.

An explanation of biblical meaning and intent is the result of true preaching. It means that the preacher will explain the meaning and intent of the biblical text in an understandable and accurate way. The issues addressed by the pastor need to flow out of the bible text. The agenda of a truly biblical message is set by the words of the Bible and nothing else. Real expositional preaching begins with an examination of God's Word.

While some of the criticism directed toward seeker-sensitive churches and their sermons are based upon misunderstanding, there are churches that have departed from preaching that is biblically based. The Bible is not the text for their sermons; it barely influences their sermons. At best, biblical content is an afterthought. The Bible is mentioned only after the case is made and the point is proved.

Types of Expositional Preaching

In my (Ed) book, Planting New Churches in a Postmodern Age, I talk about preaching. I have included some of my explanation of preaching here. There are four common types of expositional preaching: verse-by-verse, thematic, narrative, and topical. Briefly, let us examine each type.

Exposition Verse-by-Verse

Preaching verse-by-verse involves the systematic reading and explanation of a passage of the Bible. Often, this type of preaching results in a series of messages based upon a single book of the Bible. The pastor will preach through the book of James, then the book of 1 Kings, etc. While this style breaks down the meaning of each passage piece by piece, it also defines the meaning of each passage within the context of the entire biblical book being addressed.

After our earlier comments, you might think we disapprove of this form of preaching. The opposite it true. It is a great way to faithfully present the whole counsel of God. The only danger is when it is the only acceptable way.

Exposition By Theme (or Doctrine)

Thematic preaching is an excellent method to utilize when preaching on doctrinal subjects or Biblical themes. Preachers can combine the teaching of a number of Bible passages in order to address various everyday topics. For example, a speaker could present three different passages (John 14:25-27; Ephesians 2:14-18; Philippians 4:4-7) in a message series entitled "Experiencing Real Peace In A Chaotic World." The key is to be faithful to their meaning, not just using them to prove your point.

Thematic expository preaching may also involve utilizing as many as ten or twelve different scripture passages in each sermon. Since the Bible provides teaching on various themes dispersed in different books of the Bible, this style of preaching is a good way to expose people to the broad spectrum of God's Word. Also, this method helps new Christians or uninformed unbelievers learn about the general themes and consistency that can be found throughout the Bible.

This form of preaching has become more and more popular in churches in the last twenty years. It has allowed preachers to present the "full counsel" of God on a subject, drawing from a series of text throughout a message series. However, in order to do this right, many pastors have found that they need to preach an extended time. For example, a sermon series on what the Bible teaches about marriage would take many weeks—not just a short overview of a few passages. To let the Bible set the agenda means taking the time to preach a good portion of what the Bible says about the issue. That takes time.

Narrative Exposition

Narrative preaching focuses on utilizing biblical texts that tell a story. The story is the centerpiece of the message and is weaved into the entire fabric of the sermon from beginning to end.

When using this type of exposition, the preacher might relate a story from on the gospels such as Jesus feeding the five thousand (John 6). In sharing the story, the preacher seeks to draw the audience into the story as though they were part of it. As a result, those listening grasp the full meaning of Jesus' words and teachings and how they apply to every day life. Narrative preaching can be effective in the postmodern North American culture because personal stories have become the way to communicate meaning. In addition, the emerging generation appears to be rejecting traditional approaches.

I (Ed) shared this example in Planting New Churches in a Postmodern Age:

> Some time ago, I discovered the value of narrative preaching during a church-starting crusade in West Africa. Although I believed I had preached a great message on the first night of a crusade, I found that the nationals had not connected with my verse-by-verse exposition of Luke 14.
>
> On the second night, I adapted my style to use narrative exposition of the Nicodemus story from John 3. Those in attendance responded to the unfolding story with enthusiastic applause at key points. Their excitement grew. When I told of Nicodemus' presence at the foot of Jesus' cross, the crowd exploded with joy. Many responded to the gospel invitation that night. Over 100 attended the first service of the new church.[5]

It is likely that narrative expository preaching will grow more popular in this culture in the coming years. This will have a positive impact on the Church and culture as long as the narratives remain consistent with biblical texts. It will benefit the Church greatly to remember that Jesus demonstrated the effectiveness and value of narrative preaching through His use of parables.

It is likely that narrative expository preaching will grow more popular in this culture in the coming years. This will have a positive impact on the Church and culture as long as the narratives remain consistent with biblical texts. It will benefit the Church greatly to remember that Jesus demonstrated the effectiveness and value of narrative preaching through His use of parables.

I (Ed) recently visited North Point Church in Alpharetta, GA. Andy Stanley, the pastor, was preaching through the "questions" of the Pharisees: which is the greatest commandment, what happens if a wife is married

---

5. Ed Stetzer, *Planting New Churches in a Postmodern Age* (Broadman and Holman, 2003), 279.

to seven brothers, etc. He explained each story then related to our own attempts to trap God, and illustrated the foolishness of such. A series of passages that many have skimmed over Andy Stanley used to teach a tremendous truth.

For some reason, we evangelicals have often assumed that if it is not doctrinal, it does not matter. The opposite is true. About three quarters of the Bible is story and that story is life transforming, if we will not only see it as history, but also see if as instruction.

Exposition By Topic

Topical preaching usually revolves around one passage of scripture and centers on one theme. Because it is generally a single message built around one theme, it is topical. On the other hand, it is expositional because it utilizes one biblical passage as the source of its content.

This style of exposition is used most often on special occasions such as Easter, Mother's Day, Father's Day, Christmas, etc. However, usually this approach to preaching does not leave adequate time to address the full scope of God's Word like other methods can. This approach does not allow the pastor to present a full bible teaching on a subject.

In regard to the four styles of biblical preaching, this is the easiest to get off track. It can be difficult to be faithful to biblical context. It limits the preacher's ability to honestly let the bible be the foundation of the message. While it is relevant at times, preachers should use this approach to exposition on a limited basis.

Exposition & Application

Every good message starts with a primary question: What's the point? The people want to be able to grasp what the preacher is saying and they want that "point" to matter to them. However, pastors often do not answer the questions that the people in the church are asking.

If Andy Stanley had only preached on the nature of the resurrected body in relationship to their marriage mentioned above, it would have been a missed opportunity. The Pharisees really did not care—they were just trying to trap Jesus. (And, does anyone really have a good explanation for that answer from Jesus?—I don't. It's on my "things to ask" list when I get to heaven.)

If a pastor is preaching on the purpose of the plagues in Egypt while a family is thinking of splitting up, the pastor will probably miss the mark. If the pastor is explaining the importance of predestination in Ephesians while the husband is considering adultery, the pastor will probably miss the mark. Pastors need to answer the questions that people are asking and answer those questions in a way that transforms people's thinking and ultimately the way they live their lives. An effective sermon will accomplish this task if it is biblically faithful, is memorable, engages the whole person, and provides encouragement. Every message needs to encourage those listening even if it is the encouragement to miss hell.

Memorable

When a message is presented to a group of people, it should be delivered in a format that makes the point or points easily remembered. The most effective sermons are those that make a point that is simple and easy to remember. Pithy sayings are an effective tool for doing this. Jesus provides us with some examples. Each of the following statements can be easily quoted and used as "the point" of a sermon:

- Matthew 7:12 Do to others what you would have them do to you.
- Mark 3:25 If a house is divided against itself, that house cannot stand.
- Luke 6:37 Do not judge, and you will not be judged.
- 1 Corinthians 15:33 "Bad company corrupts good character."
- 2 Corinthians 3:6 "for the letter kills, but the Spirit gives life."
- 2 Thessalonians 3:10 "If a man will not work, he shall not eat."
- 1 Corinthians 5:6 "Don't you know that a little yeast works through the whole batch of dough?"

I (Ed) could always tell a lot from people's response to my messages. No one ever came to me and said, "I really appreciate you explaining why the location of Sinai is important." It is important, but it was not what people remembered. Instead, years later, my church members would quote "Hurt People, Hurt People" from my message series on relationships. It was a biblical truth put in language they could all remember.

Encourages the Whole Person

Jesus and Paul used analogies, illustrations, and object lessons to communicate their message. Jesus used bread, fish, sawdust, boards, and many other things common to the lives of the people to whom he was speaking. Paul utilized references to sports and the military in order to communicate truth in an understandable way.

In addition, speakers today have the opportunity to use tools like videos, DVD's, CD's, and PowerPoint to bring a biblical message to life. Also, speakers today should seek to find ways to touch all five senses (touch, taste, smell, sight, and hearing) in order to communicate their message effectively. Effective messages utilize good analogies, illustrations, object lessons, technology, and touch points.

Earlier, we gave the example of a church using the movie Braveheart. The problem was not the use of the movie. Sure, not any movie is appropriate. It would be a shame if children would see at church movies they are not allowed to see at home.

But the movie can be a powerful tool if it illustrates the scripture (rather than the scripture illustrating the movie). If the message is on the Bible teaching on revenge, there is nothing wrong with a video clip that illustrates the futility of revenge, or a drama and makes that point, or a testimony, any of these things can help connect with the whole person.

Encouragement

Paul often sought to engage the emotions of his hearers.[6] There is nothing wrong with engaging your listener with encouragement—and not just information. Instead of using a scholarly approach and exegetical methods to impress and amaze listeners, it would be much wiser to share personal hurts, weaknesses, and struggles through each topic together.[7] When a speaker is real and authentic about his life struggles with a congregation, people can grasp biblical truth better and really understand how it applies to everyday life—that is encouraging. For the effective preacher, being real and genuine is a critical communication issue.

Encouragement comes in many shapes and sizes. Not every message has a happy ending, but every message can encourage the listeners to do, be, act, or think. That is encouraging.

---

6. Bailey, 81.
7. John R. Claypool, The Preaching Event (San Francisco: Harper Collins, 1989), 87.

Listener Informed

If people attended church the Sunday after September 11, 2001, pastors should have addressed some aspect of that event and provided a sense of hope and encouragement in the midst of tragedy and sorrow. Some pastors probably did not mention or speak about what was on everybody's mind—why did this happen? Instead, they proceeded with their scheduled text. That is a critical time when some pastors failed to address the needs of those listening. The scriptures model a different paradigm. For example, Paul varied his message depending on the needs and spiritual conditions of the listeners. The chart below illustrates his changing style:

Text	Place	Audience	Approach
Acts 13:15-41	Antioch of Pisidia	Interested Jews	Much history and Hebrew scripture
Acts 14:15-17	Lystra	Idolaters	Nature is a bridge to the gospel
Acts 17:22-31	Athens	Educated philosophers	Quotes a Stoic poet and acknowledges their religious quest
Acts 22:3-21	Jerusalem	Mob of Jews	Gives a personal testimony[8]

What is on the mind of the people should also be on the mind of the preacher. As such, it should impact the message. If the church is going through a tough time, then it is OK to share about that—to teach what

---

8. Ed Stetzer, Planting New Churches in a Postmodern Age (Broadman and Holman, 2003), 281.

the bible says about perseverance and patience. Too often we think it is a measure of our biblical commitment that we do not let anything take us off our preaching plan. That's a false boundary.

Conclusion

Communicating biblical truth is such a critical issue in this emerging postmodern culture. It is an opportunity for the preacher to shine the light of truth in a dark and sometimes cynical world. In order to accomplish this task, messengers can utilize various styles and multiple tools of communication. The key boundary for preachers to recognize the need to preach using the Word of God as the basis and centerpiece for the message.

In regard to preaching in a church planting context, it is generally understood that the speaker's messages will not contain the same depth of biblical content in the early stages of the new church's existence. In the beginning stage, effective messages will generally be defined as evangelistic sermons. These messages contain a sharper focus, contain an understanding of the fact that the audience is less familiar with the Bible, involve less exegetical work with the biblical text, contain a simplified organizational structure, speak to real life issues, and are filled with more humor and illustrations.[9]

As the new church grows and develops, the preacher will share messages that have more depth while maintaining almost the same level of practicality apparent in the beginning stage. Even after a church develops and grows, the preaching should always be practical and relevant to its audience. This can be a difficult task at times for preachers, but they should seek to obtain and utilize as many tools as necessary to achieve this objective.

In addition, it is imperative that we not only stay immersed in scripture but also study the culture in order to be effective communicators. Exegeting the culture helps preachers understand the audience.

The purpose of an effective sermon should ultimately be encounter with God not just education.[10] As we lead people toward that encounter, we should be able to affirm with John Calvin, "I have not corrupted one single

---

9. Larry Moyer, Evangelistic Preaching in Leadership Handbooks of Practical theology. Word and Worship general editor (Grand Rapids: Baker Book House, 1992), 11.
10. Calvin Miller, Marketplace Preaching: How to Return the Sermon to Where It Belongs (Grand Rapids: Baker Book House, 1995), 142.

passage of Scripture, nor twisted it as far as I know…I have always studied to be simple…"[11]

It is encouraging to know that emerging churches are rediscovering and reemphasizing strong biblical content as they seek to experience the living God. Even though the styles and tools of delivery are changing some in this postmodern age, preaching in any age should always be, first and foremost, biblical preaching. "Preach the Word!"

QUESTIONS TO CHEW ON

1. Of all the sermons you've ever heard, which one do you remember best? Why do you remember it?

2. Of all the sermons you've ever heard, which one changed your life the most? What did it do to your thinking? Feeling? Actions? How did this sermon change you?

3. If you could tell preachers how to preach, what would you like to see included in sermons that are not there now? Why? Would your suggestions make sermons more biblical?

4. If sermons should be effective in culture, what in your culture would better influence sermons?

5. Do you like sermons that produce in you more "thinking" or "feeling"?

6. How would you preach a sermon on Jesus to get listeners to love Him more?

---

11. John Calvin cited by Stott, 128.

Chapter 8

PREACHING

A Parable

The young missionary stood in the middle of a village, surrounded by Nimo who were ready to listen to them. This was God's open door to reach the Nimo with the gospel. A young boy from the tribe had been badly chewed up by a wild boar. The missionaries had shot the boar and taken the boy back to their camp where a doctor sewed him back together, using 107 stitches. Usually, victims like this were left before their idols until they died. One of the leaders behind the older missionary told the Nimo the Christian "medicine man" made the boy live again. The old leader had stood by the table as the young boy was stitched up.

The young missionary stood in the village with the healed boy—although scarred by stitches—to tell them what had happened. He began his sermon, "Jesus healed this boy." The Nimo thought the doctor's name was Jesus.

The young missionary told how Jesus came to forgive their sins. The Nimo thought they had to go ask the mission doctor for forgiveness. The Nimo Christian who lived among the Westerners whispered in the ear of the older missionary to explain the confusion the tribal members were having with the sermon.

The older missionary interrupted and asked his younger colleague to talk to the Nimo who told of the problem in communication. The older missionary began preaching, telling the story of creation and the world around the Nimo. He explained how the Creator—God—created all these people in His image. Eventually, he told them of Jesus, the Son of God. He explained that Jesus lived in the heart of the doctor who healed the boy and that their love for Jesus had motivated them to come tell them the good news.

Doing Evangelism

The above story actually happened when I (Elmer) was ministering to a group of Laotians who left their mountain home to cross the Mekong River into Thailand in 1977. They were running from the Communists. When the preacher made several cultural mistakes, a 15 year-old boy whispered to me the problems. I asked the boy if he had ever interpreted a sermon, he said "No." I said, "You will now," and I interrupted the speaker and preached an hour sermon, telling the story of the Creator-God up to God's Son who was born of a virgin. At the end of the sermon, almost all of them were converted, baptized by an elder, and became a church fellowship with the Christian and Missionary Alliance.

Begin by Defining Evangelism

We do not develop an evangelistic strategy based on the nature of the audience, i.e., postmodernity; but rather develop a strategy beginning with the Word of God and the Great Commission. Therefore, we will begin our task by defining evangelism, then looking at the challenge of postmodernity through the eyes of the Great Commission to get a clearer understanding of what should be the Church's response.

The most succinct definition we know is from *The Practical Encyclopedia of Evangelism and Church Growth*, "Evangelism is communicating the Gospel in an understandable manner and motivating a person to respond to Christ and become a responsible member of his church." From this definition of evangelism[1], let's use the following five areas to examine what should be our approach to people living in a postmodern age.

The Gospel: What message shall we preach?

Communication: How shall we contact them?

An understandable manner: What barriers shall we overcome?

Motivating them to respond: How shall we get the message across?

Responsible members of a church: What is the Church?

Answering these five questions will not guarantee success in ministry, nor will it even give a basic set of principles to minister in a postmodern world. But these answers will suggest certain presuppositions that can guide future ministry.

---

1. Donald A. McGavran and Winfield C. Arn, Ten Steps for Church Growth (San Francisco: HarperSanFrancisco, 1977), 51 quoted in Elmer L. Towns, Practical Encyclopedia of Evangelism and Church Growth, (Ventura, CA: Regal Books, 1995), 214.

THE GOSPEL: WHAT MESSAGE SHALL WE PREACH?

In philosophical postmodernism, words do not have meaning. Words only mean what current users attribute to them. Truth is not eternal, and it is certainly not decided by the modern scientific method, i.e., the way civilization has done it; nor do they accept truth from any religious sources. Truth is relative, and it has the meaning that has (a) been agreed upon, (b) or has been attributed by a user. Therefore, if the postmodernist view of words and truth is correct, much of biblical Christianity collapses, because there would be no standardized meaning. But Christianity is grounded in objective truth that was established in historical objectivity.

However, we have an "everlasting gospel to preach" (Rev. 14:6) and "His truth endures to all generations" (Ps. 100:5). God is eternal and does not change; His message is the same from one generation to another, and from one changing culture to another.

The gospel content is the message of the death, burial and resurrection of Jesus Christ (1 Cor. 15:1-3). This is called the *propositional truth of the gospel*, i.e., that which is true in all cultures and in all ages. These eternal truths are the principles of salvation. But the Gospel is also a person; it is Jesus Christ, i.e., this is the *personal gospel*. Jesus is the message of evangelism. "There is no other name . . . by which we must be saved" (Acts 4:12). Whereas some today may reject the principles of Christianity, they must accept the personal gospel; because that is the methodology he uses to arrive at truth.

The average person today rejects the Church for its hypocrisy, lethargy, or for its abuses. And many times the skeptic is not without justification in rejecting the Church, because many local churches operate on earth as a man-driven organization not a God-driven organization. So, when the postmodern world attacks the church, make sure you are not defending a church or denomination that doesn't deserve defending.

Ironically, the postmodern who rejects the contemporary Church would probably like its founder, Jesus Christ. Jesus was as anti-bureaucratic as they are. He condemned religious shams of His age, as they condemn the religious shams of our age. Jesus was anti-bureaucratic in both His teaching and His life, as is the postmodern. In every sense of the word, Jesus was a revolutionary. But the problem is the revolution that Jesus began against the dead religions of His day, ultimately has been "encapsulated" in many dead spiritual institutions of our day. Today, Jesus wouldn't like a lot of the churches that we call "church" because these churches do not represent the body He founded.

So remember, the Church is called His Body (1 Cor. 12:27), and it must represent Jesus on this earth. However, the visible Church is subject to the limitations of humanity, as was the physical body of Jesus. But at the same time the Church is very much divine in its supernatural authority and power, as Jesus in His earthly body was the God-Man. So the Church must be both human and divine, an organism and an organization; but many times it is not. So, what is our first step of outreach? To evangelize people in today's world, the local church must become the spiritual Church as intended by Jesus (Matt. 16:18). This means the Church must experience God's love, peace, joy, patience, gentleness, good works, faith, meekness and self-control. (See Gal. 5:22-23).

Historically, the power of God through local churches has overcome every kind of opposition for approximately 2000 years. Therefore, we should not fear any new evangelistic paradigm or any new methods we need to employ to reach emerging postmodern generations. The Church and its gospel message will endure, and the Church will always be in conflict with culture. However, whether the Church will endure as a stronger or weaker institution is not yet seen, nor is it seen whether its conflict with culture will become more intense, or not.

> **Evangelism is communicating the Gospel in an understandable manner and motivating a person to respond to Christ and become a responsible member of his church.**

But let's go back and examine who we are and what we've done. In the past decades, the Church has only been moderately successful in evangelizing America that was dominated by modern thinking. Even though America has a Protestant-Puritan ethic, and our nation is described as having a Judeo-Christian culture, our evangelism in America as "one nation under God" has only been moderately successful. What will happen when American society becomes even more postmodern and post-Christian (or anti-Christian)? That question means what will happen when America becomes less Christian?

Will the Church become more successful in a different cultural paradigm when we have to confront the restraints of a new and different cultural "glue," i.e., postmodernity? Many think the Church will becomes less successful in preaching the gospel to postmoderns, unless it makes the

Church a "postmodern church." Must we sever our emotional umbilical cord to modernity and embrace postmodernity? Won't that be just as bad as when the church tried to be trendy and modern in the 1980s?

Our question, "What message shall we preach?", has an answer. Thom Wolf, the former pastor at the Church on Brady in Los Angeles says, "The central issue of communicating the message of Christ will be on the person of Christ, and the uniqueness of the resurrection."[2]

We must preach "the gospel of Christ . . . is the power of God to salvation" (Rom. 1:16).

COMMUNICATION: HOW SHALL WE CONTACT THEM?

Years ago Francis Schaefer, an evangelical apologetic guru, asked a question in a book, "How then shall we live?" But today's question is, "How now shall we communicate the gospel?" God gave us the gospel in words, but now we are immersed into a culture that changes the meaning of words, and we deal with ideas that have no objective reality, and we are attacked by relevant morality and pluralistic suggestions of salvation; what is our response?

In the previous world of Western civilization, we responded with *argument absurdium*. Either you believe the truth of Christianity, or you must accept the opposite alternative of atheism and/or agnosticism. But in today's society, postmodernity has challenged the basis of the way we think and the way we argue. They say both are true at the same time. We will be forced to minister in a non-civilized environment characterized by diversity of meaning, diversity of morality, diversity of interpretation, and no "glue" to hold the "rational civilization" together. Rather than throwing up our arms in defeat, Goetz says, "Postmodernism, for all its confusion, seems just one more opportunity for the church to do what it does best—be the church."[3] Goetz's article has an excellent discussion on the death of rationalism, the death of ideology, rejection of authority, i.e., the death of civilization.

---

2. As quoted by Will McRaney in his article, "The Evangelistic Conversation in an Increasingly Postmodern America," Journal of the American Society of Church Growth, Vol. 12, 2001), 90, quoting a paper entitled "Post Modernity and the Urban Church Agenda" that Thom Wolf gave at the American Society for Church Growth Annual Conference, November 1997, Orlando, Florida.
3. As quoted by David L. Goetz, "The Riddle of Our Postmodern Culture: What is Postmodernism? Should We Even Care?", Leadership (Winter, 1997) : 56.

When we seek to evangelize the postmodern, let's not resort to dealing with external issues such as should we use alternative music in worship? Should we use PowerPoint in preaching? And what should be our approach to casual dress in worship services? These are "band-aid" approaches to the conflicts of two opposing cultural paradigms.

At the heart of the postmodern person is relationship and authentic connections. So we must learn how to connect to them as people, to deal with their real needs without compromising our message. Let's forget about our "marketing" mentality, and let's not call them "consumers." Let's not design a worship service like the world designs menus to appeal to postmodern appetites. But rather, let's pray for them to be convicted of their separation from God—their spiritual lostness. Then, let's pray for the power of the Spirit to be poured out upon the preaching of the Gospel (Acts 2:17). Let's drop the cultural presuppositions of our modernity, and invite them to follow Jesus Christ. Remember His invitation was, "Follow Me" (John 1:43).

The Church must not major on obeying rules, creating institutionalized creeds, using condescending advertisements, and employing past-culturally biased images. We must even forget about advertising. I (Elmer) once said in 1969 to a Greater Chicago ministerial association, "We must sell Jesus as the world sells Coca-Cola." I was "beat up" verbally by the pastors in the following discussion because they thought I was dealing with principles of evangelism, when actually I was suggesting we become aggressive in using our methods to get the message out. (The problem was a confusion of principles and methods). But today, I would reject the commercial attitude of selling or advertising Jesus Christ. The Church must live and preach Jesus Christ.

George Hunter tells us that "today's churches are, for the most part, waiting for the barbarians to somehow find us and our institutional setting. Consequently, we are missing out on one of the greatest "apostolic adventures" available to Christians."[4] He's right. We must go to them personally with the message of Jesus Christ.

---

4. George Hunter, The Celtic Way of Evangelism: How Christianity Can Reach the West Again (Abingdon: Nashville, 2000), 21, 121.

AN UNDERSTANDABLE MANNER: WHAT BARRIERS SHALL WE OVERCOME?

Every time we think of evangelizing, we must think of the barriers, opposition, or difficulties in presenting the gospel. Obviously, Church Growth has given us an understanding of E-0 to E-3 barriers.[5] The E-0 barrier describes evangelizing those who are already in the Church, i.e., unsaved children born in the Church or those who have transferred in their membership but have not experienced conversion. The E-1 "stained-glass" barrier describes the difficulties of external things that keep people from becoming saved or even attending our churches, i.e., location, facilities, name, lack of equipment, and lack of services. E-2 are the cultural and class barriers that hinder the presentation of the gospel to people in their ethnic customs or culture. We must communicate the gospel "cross-culturally" so that the people hear and properly understand the message of Jesus Christ. As Donald McGavran has said, "People like to become Christians without having to cross racial, linguistic, or class barriers."[6] Finally, E-3 is a language barrier.

Again, McGavran said, "Each man likes to hear the Gospel in his own heart-language."[7] This means that people respond to the gospel when it is preached to them in the language of their heart, or the language by which they think, i.e., not just a trade language.

Barriers to Evangelism
E-1 *Stained Glass Barrier*: an outward thing that keeps the unsaved from hearing the gospel.
E-2 *Cultural and Class Barrier*: the cultural, class, or ethnic differences that make it difficult to communicate the gospel.
E-3 *Language Barrier*: differences in dialect or language that make it difficult to communicate the gospel.

We may find persons in a postmodern age actually has fewer barriers to evangelism than person did in modernity. While they have different meanings to words, values, and orientation to life; look at the

---

5. Elmer L. Towns, Ed., "Evangelism: E-1, E-2, E-3," A Practical Encyclopedia of Evangelism and Church Growth (Ventura, CA: Regal Books, 1995), 206.
6. Donald A. McGavran, as cited by Elmer L. Towns, Practical Encyclopedia: Evangelism and Church Growth (Ventura, CA: Regal Books, 1995), 264.
7. Ibid.

postmodern as he or she encounters Jesus Christ. First, people today acknowledge the supernatural and mystery of God. Second, they prize relationships. Remember Christianity is a relationship between them and God. Third, they value experience. Christianity is not head belief, nor is it just doctrine and creeds. But conversion is an experience that will transform their life when they become new creatures in Jesus Christ (2 Cor. 5:17). Fourth, they think viscerally, not linearly. Since the viscera is the body cavity and they think with their total being, this is a truer picture of the New Testament concept of belief. Belief involves a total response of the person, i.e., intellect, emotion, and will, including self-perception and self-direction. The way to reach the people today is to call them to a New Testament concept of belief in Jesus Christ.

MOTIVATING THEM TO RESPOND: HOW SHALL WE GET THE MESSAGE ACROSS?

The Church must not be afraid of its strength. By that is meant the Church must not be afraid of the supernatural, i.e., power evangelism, prayer intervention, deliverance, transformation, and miracles.[8] The church of modernity is reflected in rationality, formula, and doctrine; but the Church that will be effective in a postmodern world must be both doctrinally based and unafraid of living our biblical experiences. It must operate in the realm of the natural and the supernatural. We must present the gospel to people, challenging them to a relationship with the Creator of the universe, not to just join a church and accept the rules of Christianity. Our challenge is not just to help people accept the objective truth of Christianity; our challenge is to help postmodern people experience the life of God and relate personally to Jesus Christ, so they can experience eternal life.

Because God meets people where they are, let's not be surprised if God uses different methods today. He works differently today than he did in the past age. As an illustration, God used apologetics, rational presentation, and logic when ministering to people who lived in our rational Western

---

8. While we believe the day of sign-miracles has passed, i.e., the ability to do miracles as a demonstrative sign to validate the message of Christianity, we do not believe the day of miracles has passed. Every answer to prayer is a miracle, just as every healing. And then God does "epochs," which means God intervenes in the affairs of life, God delivers people from addiction, God transforms every part of a person's life, i.e., thinking, feeling, desires, and self-perceptions. Christianity is both rational and experiential.

civilization. We should not be surprised when God uses the supernatural, i.e., mystery, power evangelism and experiential praise worship to confront a postmodern world that does not think as logically as past generations, but appreciates experiential justification of its conclusions. This is not to say that we look for experience for its own sake. Rather, we recognize the authority of scripture and understand that the scriptures speak of certain experiences. We should embrace such biblical practices in the same way we embrace biblical doctrine..

As a matter of fact, our traditional methods will not be as effective in the future, as they have been in the past. No one method of communicating the gospel will always be effective. Those who minister to the postmodern mention the following methods: narratives, parables, creative worship, testimonies, drama, small groups (cells), dialogue, answering questions and experiencing community.

> Methods are many,
> Principles are few.
> Methods may change,
> But principles never do.
>
> Anon.

Methods represent a change in style. In other words, witnessing to emerging generations requires a different approach. It will be different than the methods of the past. There is a need to employ a postmodern evangelistic strategy as churches share the unchanging gospel.

Consequently, there are several principles that will help any church or individual develop an effective evangelistic approach in this postmodern age. First, evangelism needs to be understood as a process not an event. Second, evangelism needs to be relational or community-oriented. Third, evangelism needs to involve more listening on the part of the witness. Fourth, evangelism needs to have a foundation of effective prayer.[9]

---

9. Ed Stetzer, Planting New Churches in a Postmodern Age (Nashville, TN: Broadman & Holman Publishers, 2003). Much of the material that follows comes from Planting New Churches in a Postmodern Age.

Process Evangelism

When evangelism is seen as a process rather than a one-time event, it takes some pressure off of the witness and the potential believer. The witness does not have to feel like a failure when every witnessing opportunity does not result in a conversion. Also, the person being witnessed to does not perceive pressure to make a decision on the spot unless they are ready to do so. Then, each encounter with an unbeliever is part of a journey to faith in Christ. The destination of conversion will hopefully occur at some point, but effective evangelism is often progressive in nature.

In addition, there is no guarantee that individuals are immediately ready to respond to the gospel. There are people in North America today who have never heard the gospel, seen a Bible, or heard the name of Jesus. To expect uninformed unbelievers to immediately respond to someone asking them to "Repent, believe, and ask Jesus into your heart" can be short-sighted. Churches should not assume that people understand the basic tenets of the gospel nor who God is, even in this society.

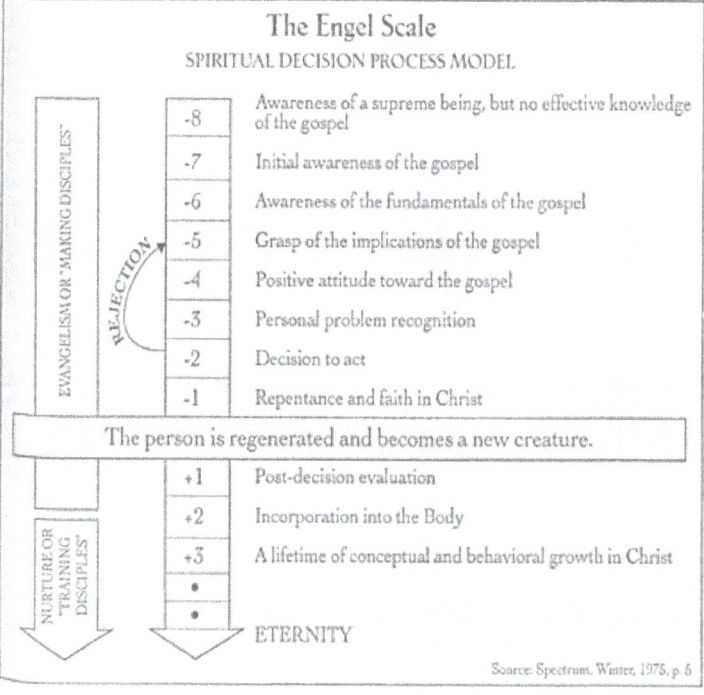

One excellent tool for helping the planter understand people's spiritual awareness is the Engel scale.[10] This linear scale, which resembles a number line, depicts a series of steps from complete unawareness and ignorance of the gospel to a maturing commitment to Christianity.

Applying The Engel Scale

The Engel Scale classifies awareness of the gospel in a range of steps from -8 to +3, as follows:

-8: Awareness of a supreme being but no effective knowledge of the gospel

-7: Initial awareness of the gospel

-6: Awareness of the fundamentals of the gospel

-5: Grasp of implications of the gospel

-4: Positive attitude toward the gospel

-3: Counting the cost

-2: Decision to act

-1: Repentance and faith in Christ

REGENERATION

+1: Post-decision evaluation

+2: Incorporation into the body

+3: A lifetime of growth in Christ—discipleship and service

Negative one, repentance and faith in Christ, is the crucial step, but not necessarily an isolated event. It is built upon a patient process. God can make repentance and faith in Christ an instantaneous event, but it is usually a process which leads to this event.[11] Following conversion (step 0), the new believer begins to evaluate the decision, is incorporated into a fellowship of believers, and becomes one who actively shares the gospel. The evangelist's task is to partner with God in order to move people toward understanding the gospel—toward the point of repentance and faith in Christ. The effective evangelist will learn to recognize that people are at different stages when they come to worship services.

In this partnership process, the soul winner may meet an individual who seems to stand at –6. The wise Christian will not rush into the reasons

---

10. There are different versions of the Engel scale. Malphurs describes a slightly different version than I (Elmer) have reproduced (Aubrey Malphurs, Planting Growing Churches for the 21st Century (Grand Rapids, MI: Baker Book House, 1992), 275.

11. Engel erroneously places repentance before regeneration. Some theologians have historically held that regeneration precedes (and enables) repentance.

the Bible says we need Christ for such an approach assumes that person believes in the authority of scripture and its personal application to his or her life. A better approach at that time might be to share biblical passages that can help the non-Christian understand more about Christianity. Before a person can make an intelligent choice for the gospel, he or she must know what the gospel means. Jesus encouraged men and women to "count the cost."

Also, effective evangelism recognizes that people are at different levels of spiritual awareness and attitude. One person may be completely unaware of spiritual things from a biblical perspective, but that individual also has a desire or a willingness to learn. Another person may have some knowledge of God, the Bible, and the gospel, but that individual is close-minded about making a decision to repent and receive Jesus Christ as personal Lord and Savior. Effective evangelism takes all of this into account and recognizes that people are at different stages. The task becomes learning to partner with God in order to influence people toward understanding and responding to the gospel.

One tool that can help us understand evangelism as a process is the Gray Matrix.[12] It is a modification of an older tool called the Engel Scale. Here are some practical ways in which this matrix can assist in evangelistic efforts:

- Anything which moves people from left to right across the scale is 'evangelistic'. This might include acts of service and friendship, mum and baby clubs, medical and development work—many things which are not apparently 'preaching'. Yet in fact, the word Jesus used when he told us to 'preach the Gospel' has a much wider meaning than speech—it refers to communication.
- If we can understand roughly where a single person or target group of people is situated on the scale, we can choose an appropriate approach to reach them.
- If people are near the bottom of the scale, we must not use Christian language and ideas which will mean

---

12. www.thegraymatrix.info/.

nothing to them. We must assess our message through their eyes, not ours. It may also be inappropriate to heavily 'preach for a decision' at this point.

- Pressures of society and culture, and the strategies of the Enemy, will tend to pull people down towards the bottom left-hand of the scale. God's purpose is to draw people to the top right-hand side by His Spirit, through the witness of his people.[13]

The person who effectively shares his or her faith recognizes that people are at different stages of openness and knowledge. In Planting New Churches in a Postmodern Age, I gave this example:

> (O)ne young woman in a former pastorate came to church and was crying by the end of worship. Speaking with me after the service she said, "I know I need to receive Christ into my heart because I'm separated from Him." She stood at the point of conversion. All I had to do was offer her assistance in taking the step of faith. On the other hand, when I served a Chinese church, I encountered many people who had no awareness of Christianity. I began evangelizing them by teaching the existence of God as displayed in the scriptures.[14]

The Gray Matrix also show a sobering reality. People are further back on the scale than they were twenty, fifty, or one hundred years ago. We start further back, so our message must start at a different point, lest we miss the hearer.

Relational Evangelism

While the Gray Matrix is helpful, it does not provide all the insight needed to develop an effective evangelism strategy. Evangelism in this emerging world needs to be relational. Ray Jones, personal evangelism specialist at the North American Mission Board, states:

> Effectively reaching postmoderns with the truth of the gospel will occur only if Christians personally invest their lives in

---

13. 13 http://www.brigada.org/today/articles/gray-matrix.html.
14. 14 Dr. Edward Stetzer, Planting New Churches in a Postmodern Age (Nashville: Broadman & Holman, 2003), 190.

those left empty by the materialism of the 20th century. They want to know that you're the real deal. They want to know that you're not just after them as an evangelistic headhunter.

Relationships are huge to postmoderns. If you can develop and cultivate relationships, you're going to go a long way to being able to reach postmoderns.[15]

Therefore, effective evangelism involves finding touch points in people's lives in order to build relational bridges. As this occurs, there will be opportunities to discover the spiritual awareness and attitude level of the potential believer and begin to share biblical truth and spiritual journey experiences. Touch points could involve any number of possibilities—noticing a hobby, sending a birthday card, performing a random act of kindness, acknowledging a major accomplishment, etc. Building relational bridges needs to become part of everyday life.[16]

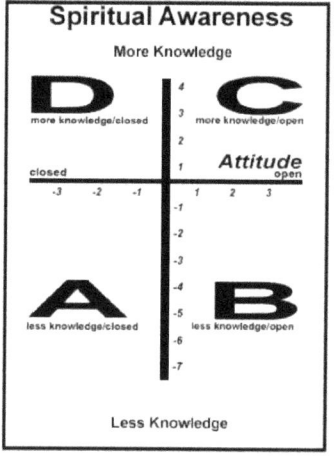

This relational principle also has ramifications for the community of believers as well. In regard to this, I would like to suggest the "Stetzer Evangelism Journey." This combines the ideas of the Engel Scale and the Gray Matrix. There are also some additional insights about spiritual journey included from Darrell Gruder's book *The Missional Church*.[17]

There are two conversions—one temporal and one eternal. The first conversion is the **conversion to community**. With few exceptions, people come to Christ after they have journeyed with other Christians—examining them and considering their claims. They can come into community at any point. Thus, the funnel-shaped lines (representing community) stretch all the way to the top of the diagram. At any point, a person can decide to begin a spiritual journey toward Christ.

---

15. Lee Weeks, "Postmoderns extremely receptive to the gospel, says evangelism head of the Southern Baptist North American Mission Board," Baptist Press article, 20 October, 2000.
16. W. Oscar Thompson, Jr., Concentric Circles of Concern (Nashville: Broadman Press, 1981), 124-125.
17. Darrell L. Guder (Editor), and Lois Barrett, Missional Church: A Vision for the Sending of the Church in North America (Grand Rapids, MI: William B. Eerdmans Publishing Co., 1998).

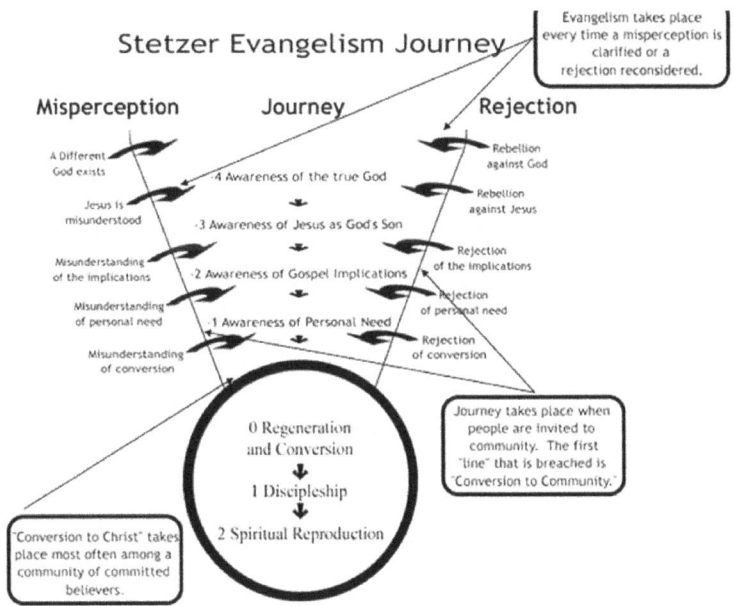

The circle represents the Church. Church and Christian community must not be the same thing. Unbelievers can and should be invited into the community, but they are not part of the Church. A church is a body of believers (more on that later). A person becomes part of the Church with the second and eternal conversion, the **conversion to Christ**.

Each curved arrow is representative of evangelism. For example, a person who has rejected God and who is living in rebellion can be challenged to live a different kind of life by a committed believer. In this context, the lost person can decide to consider the validity of a just God in conversation with their Christian friends. They may begin to believe that God is real and may then consider the claims of Christ. At some point, they begin to consider these things in community with believers.[18]

Listening Evangelism

Traditionally, evangelizing has involved seeking to share the gospel as quickly and as thoroughly as possible with a potential believer and leading that person to pray to receive Christ on the spot. This method does not necessarily take into consideration the varying levels of spiritual awareness and attitude that are possible from person to person. One way to address

---

18. Stetzer, 193.

this issue is to learn to be more sensitive to people and listen to them before jumping right into a canned gospel presentation.

In a recent seminar on postmodern ministry, one of the seminar leaders suggested that the most effective method of evangelization that can be used by churches today is listening evangelism. In other words, if church leaders want to teach people to evangelize, teach people how to observe and listen carefully to potential believers.

To illustrate this point, the speaker told the story of how he had attempted to witness to a person who was very knowledgeable about spiritual and religious things. All the unbeliever did was argue each point. Later, a young lady who was also a new believer was able to lead this man to Christ because she noticed how unhappy this unbeliever was and identified with his loneliness. That young believer responded by sharing how Jesus Christ came into her life, and she no longer feels lonely. That led the unbeliever to respond to Christ.[19]

Praying Evangelism

Finally, effective evangelism in the postmodern age requires effective prayer. This can be taken for granted in the rush to get things done, but prayer can be a powerful tool in evangelism. Several years ago, David Macfarlane suggested five prayers that are still relevant for evangelism in our postmodern age:

> Prayer No. 1: "Lord, keep me alert and sensitive to the opportunities You are bring my way today."
>
> Prayer No. 2: "Lord, here I am. I am ready for You to use me today."
>
> Prayer No. 3: "Lord, help me to be creative so that I can take advantage of the opportunities around me to make an impact on others for Christ."
>
> Prayer No. 4: "Now, Lord consider their threats and enable your servants to speak your word with great boldness."

---

19. CCN Leadership Training Series, "Post Modern Ministry: Awakening to the New Reality," May 6, 2003. www.ccnonline.net..

Prayer No. 5: "Lord, keep me faithful even when I do not see the results right away."[20]

When all of these principles of evangelism begin to work together, God can produce some meaningful results. About a year ago, my (Ed) friend Mike Dodson had the privilege of traveling to a European country with a team of people on a mission trip. On this trip, they assisted a group of missionaries in reaching out to immigrants mainly from Muslim countries.

There was one young man that "connected" with Mike at one of the outreach events. As they talked for several hours, they discussed the differences between the God of Islam and the God of the Bible. This encounter did not lead to a conversion to Christ of the young Muslim man (that happened several days later with one of the missionaries), but Mike was excited to be part of the process of evangelism. There was an opportunity to build a relational bridge with his new Muslim friend and see and hear a movement toward Christ. That happened because my friend listened to that immigrant share about his life. Most importantly, there were many people praying for the mission trip team, and that morning my friend had fervently prayed for God to give him a divine encounter that day. God provided one.

QUESTIONS TO CHEW ON

1. Since Jesus Christ is real and the gospel is supernatural, why can't we just forget "culture" and preach the gospel to people?

2. If people do not understand the words we use to preach the gospel, how can we communicate the correct meaning to them?

3. What questions are raised in your immediate community by people who do not understand the gospel?

4. Where are most people you know on the journey? Use the Stetzer Evangelism Journey to talk about your community.

---

20. David A. Macfarlane, "Creative Evangelism—Getting Out of the Rut," Decision Magazine: March 1993, 15-16

5. If we can't use the words of scripture to preach the gospel, how can we communicate the meaning of these words to listeners?

6. If the postmodern doesn't want to think rationally or literally about God, how can we present the gospel to them?

7. Since conversion always ends with a person making a decision about Jesus Christ, how can we bring postmoderns to that decision?

Chapter 9

Christianity in a Postmodern World

A Parable

The two missionaries worked close to the fire; its warmth gave them comfort, its light gave them illumination. They scurried around the campsite getting everything ready for their rest and their continued journey. The older missionary gave the directions; the young man feverishly followed the orders because he feared the darkness.

"Has the darkness always been this threatening," the younger missionary asked.

"Yes."

"Have you always prepared the campsite like this," a second question.

"Yes."

"Does the darkness scare you?" The younger missionary was inquisitive while his older advisor seemed irritated with the questions. Then the older missionary answered, "The darkness has always been threatening, that's why we prepare for the night as we do."

Then it began to rain—hard rain—harder than it had ever rained before. Usually the jungle was watered with a nightly mist, but tonight the older missionary didn't know how to cope with sheets of rain. They didn't have a tent; it had never been needed. They didn't have parkas; they were not needed.

The fire popped and sizzled as the rain fell on the red-hot coals. At first the heat evaporated the raindrops. But with each evaporating drop of rain, the coals lost their heat; the red glow dimmed.

"*Put more wood on the fire,*" the old missionary yelled. "*We can't let the fire go out.*" But the new wood was wet; it only steamed in the dying flames. They piled more wood onto the fire, but that was not the answer.

The frustrated younger missionary yelled, "*We should have brought plastic to keep the wood dry.*" The older missionary shrugged his shoulders, "*We've never had any problems with rain.*"

The fire flickered its last and darkness enveloped the two missionaries. They fumbled for their possessions, trying to get everything under a tree for protection. "*I should have built the fire in a cave or under a tree,*" the old missionary shrugged, "*but we never needed a cave.*"

The two men agreed to huddle under the thickest leaves they could find, but cover was difficult to find without light. They agreed. "*When the morning comes, we'll dry out.*"

But they forgot the light gave them protection from the jungle predators. Then a growl penetrating the darkness reminded them of the jungle dangers. The growl was closer than ever before. If they didn't have light for protection, how could they be safe?

"*Quick, climb a tree,*" the older voice commanded. He inwardly reasoned, "*Most predators don't climb trees.*"

The two travelers sat precariously on wet slippery tree limbs, waiting fearfully for morning's light. Even if they lost all their belongings, all they wanted to do was make it to sun up. They prayed.

A Post-Christian World

Today's Church faces a new rainstorm—a new environment called postmodernity. And like our two travelers in the jungle, the Church hasn't prepared for postmodernity because (1) the Church didn't see postmodernity coming; it never before faced that cultural condition; (2) the Church doesn't know how to react in the rainstorm; postmodernity is a different worldview and a new challenge; (3) the evangelical Church is more suited to engaging a modern world and is losing ground in a postmodern world.

Even though we do not claim America was ever a truly "Christian nation," she is not now as Christian as she used to be. Notice the things we've lost, i.e., prayer in public schools, prayer at the commencement of public educational institutions, posting the Ten Commandments in public schools, the non-recognition of Christian holidays, elimination of Christian symbols in public places, increased restrictions on churches (i.e., zoning laws, door-to-door visitation, etc.), the re-interpretation of history in textbooks and media to eliminate references to the past influences of Christianity, increased liberty of Christian taboos (cursing, gambling, alcohol use, etc.), the politically correct philosophy for the Church to ordain homosexuals, the re-translation of the Bible to include gender correctness. This list only warns us of the obvious sins. What about a growing public hostility toward Christianity? With a change from a positive public attitude toward the Church to a negative attitude, what is the future?

For those who don't think there's been a change, note the following. Fifty years ago no business would have planned a company picnic or business convention on Sunday. It feared a backlash from church members. And no children's sports leagues were scheduled on Sunday morning. No movies would have shown explicit sexual intercourse, sex scenes, or sex scenes involving children. But today without the restraints of the Church and America's past Judeo-Christian value system, gambling is a nationwide scourge on the poor, divorce is at an all-time high and drug and alcohol abuse continues.

Again, look at our picture of the Church as a campfire in a primeval jungle. The fire is going out. What will it take to stoke it up again? The travelers in the jungle seem helpless. Most Christians don't believe the light will be as bright in future America as it has been in the past. What is the individual Christian doing about the dying fire? What is the individual church doing to stoke up the fire? No one seems to know what to do. Both the average Christian and the average church are just hanging on. They're trying to adjust to living in less light.

As a result of the radical changes in our culture, the Church has been caught off guard—unprepared to respond to the tremendous shifts in the way people think and live their lives. If the Church is going to respond effectively to postmodernity, there is a need to answer three basic questions. What is postmodernity? How does it differ from modernity? Then, how should the Church respond to this unexpected rainstorm?

Postmodernity involves radical change—"especially from what has been accepted as morally, ethically or spiritually correct."[1] Therefore, postmodernity is a system or way of thinking as well as a lifestyle. As a result, we

---

1. Henry Blackaby, "Postmodernism: Is It A Fad Or Here To Stay?" On Mission, September-October 2002, 16.

can distinguish between philosophical or academic postmodernism and cultural postmodernism.

Although academic postmodernism is, at its core, a moral vacuum, cultural postmodernism has some elements that prepare people for the gospel. Postmodernity is not a reason to panic. Christianity started in a pre-modern world that looked similar to our today. The church was able to proclaim its exclusive truth in a pluralistic world and it thrived.

Cultures always change. Yet, , "Just as God is a missionary God, so the church is to be a missionary church."[2] Jesus explained, "As the Father has sent Me, I also send you" (John 20:21, NKJV). Our job is to go to this new worldview and to "face a fundamental challenge. That challenge is to learn to think about (our) culture in missional terms."[3] We are missionaries on a postmodern mission field.

What, then, is postmodernity?[4] As mentioned earlier, it is important to first explore the distinction between the people and the philosophy. "Post-moderns" are one thing; the academic philosophy of "postmodernism" is not the same.

Academic and philosophical postmodernism are, by their nature, opposed to the gospel. Postmodern philosophers like Derrida, Foucalt, Rorty, and Lyotard all taught about the emptiness of existence and the meaningless nature of religion, etc. Such a system is hostile to the gospel.

As such, there is no such thing as a "postmodern church." In the technical sense, the words are oxymorons—two opposed ideas that cannot be held in common. However, most Americans have no concept of philosophical postmodernism. Instead, they just live in this postmodern culture.

> Our concern is with reaching postmodern **persons**—people who have been born into this postmodern-influenced world and are trying their best to make sense of it. It's really no different from any cross-cultural missions experience. If we seek to reach Buddhists who grew up in a Buddhist world, we must communicate with them where they are. Our relationship

---

2. Craig Van Gelder, The Essence of the Church (Grand Rapids, MI: Baker Books, 2000), 98.
3. Wilbert R. Shenk, Write the Vision (Harrisburg, PA: Trinity Press International, 1995), 43.
4. Stetzer, Planting New Churches in a Postmodern Age. Much of the following comes from Planting New Churches in a Postmodern Age.

to the postmodern world must be one of communication, not compromise.⁵

As we mentioned, some of the shifts from modernity to postmodernity are beneficial. These shifts leave open the door of opportunity for the true Church to engage postmoderns. Postmodernity has made a shift to:
1. Relationship over task.
2. Journey over destination.
3. Authenticity over excellence.
4. Experience over proposition.
5. Mystery over solution.
6. Diversity over uniformity.⁶

Cultural postmodernism seeks to discard the lies of modernity—that happiness could be found in materialism, that fulfillment would be found in progress, and the man was basically good.

Before Understanding Postmodernism, We Need To Know Modernism

Millard Erickson explains that modernism was based on
- naturalism (reality is restricted to what can be observed or proved),
- humanism (humanity is the pinnacle of the universe),
- the scientific method (knowledge is inherently good and is attainable),
- reductionism (humans are highly developed animals),
- progress (because knowledge is good, its acquisition will lead to progress),
- nature (evolution—not a creator—is responsible for life and its development),
- certainty (because knowledge is objective, we can know things for certain),
- determinism (the belief that things happened because of fixed causes),

---
5. Stetzer, 118.
6. "Post Modern Ministry: Awakening to the New Reality," CCN Leadership Training Series. Leadership Training Seminar May 6, 2003.

- individualism (the supremacy of each individual and their ability to discern truth), and
- anti-authoritarianism (each person was the final arbiter of truth).[7]

The shift to postmodernity was caused by the failure of modernity. While mankind showed great progress in the Enlightenment era, mankind has also displayed the ability to destroy life with World War I and mustard gas, World War II and the concentration camps, the threat of nuclear destruction, Oklahoma City and domestic terrorism, and the World Trade Center and international terrorism. As a result, people lost hope in the ideals of the Enlightenment, and postmodernity has arrived in the wake of the modernity dam bursting.

Literally, postmodernism is defined as "that which comes after modernism." From that definition, it follows that much of what has become postmodernism developed as a reaction to the emptiness of modernism. Thus, the common culture of our society has been permeated with the philosophical tenets of postmodernity.

Postmodernity

Postmodernism simply means, "that which comes after modernism." Understandably, much of what defines postmodernism is a reaction to modernism. Millard Erikson defines postmodernism as follows:

- the denial of personal objectivity,
- the uncertainly of knowledge,
- the death of any all-inclusive explanation,
- the denial of the inherent goodness of knowledge,
- the rejection of progress,
- the supremacy of community-based knowledge, and
- the disbelief in objective inquiry.[8]

However, it is important to recognize that the typical person in society does not discuss or consciously think about "the denial of personal objectivity." But, the typical person believes that "everybody has their own

---

7. Millard J. Erickson, Postmodernizing the Faith: Evangelical Responses to the Challenge of Postmodernism (Grand Rapids: Baker Book House, 1998), 17.
8. Millard J. Erickson, Postmodernizing the Faith: Evangelical Responses to the Challenge of Postmodernism (Grand Rapids: Baker Book House, 1998), 19.

point of view and all are equally valid." In other words, the average person does not knowingly subscribe to academic/philosophical postmodernism, but those values show up every day in postmodern culture.

In Planting New Churches in a Postmodern Age, I (Ed) compared academic/philosophical postmodernism to its cultural counterpart as follows:

Erickson's Description	**Cultural Expression**
denial of personal objectivity,	I do believe in God but that is really the influence of my parents. Nobody can know for sure.
uncertainty of knowledge,	The government says that the Atkins diet does not work, but who really knows if it is true.
death of any all-inclusive explanation,	You know, things just don't fit into a nice neat explanation
denial of knowledge's inherent goodness,	The more knowledge that is out there, the more dangerous the world is becoming.
rejection of progress,	I have all this technology but am still not happy.
supremacy of community-based knowledge,	It is arrogant to think I, alone, have figured out spiritual truth.
disbelief in objective inquiry.	Here is what I think that verse means, but I could be wrong—what is your interpretation?[9]

Four things will help you understand the spread of postmodernity: the interstate, the Internet, the cell phone, and the television. *Interstate* represents transportation so that in the today's world, almost anyone can go almost anywhere, can experience almost anything, with no boundaries. The *Internet* represents the explosive amount of knowledge and media influence so almost anyone can know just about anything about everything

---

9. Stetzer, 118.

(including definitions of words and encyclopedia data), plus be entertained by the same Internet media. The *cell phone* represents communication. Almost anyone can communicate with almost anyone, at any time, from any place. The *television* influences what we think about the meaning of life and the measure of truth.

Postmodernism has not permeated every aspect of our society. There are still many churches that cling to a "modern" way of doing things. In my (Ed) book, *Planting New Churches in a Postmodern Age*, I prepared this graph to show how the Church is functioning in the midst of postmodernism:

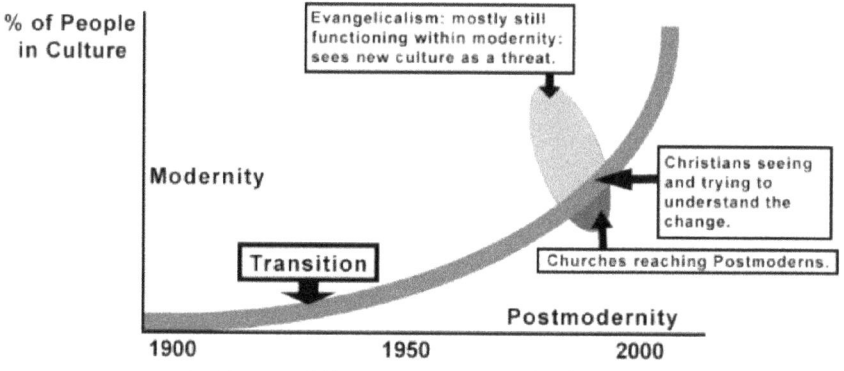

The Church can respond to the influences of postmodernity in at least four different ways. First, it can ignore it, or dismiss it as thought it is nothing. J. I. Packer, theologian at Regents College said, "Postmodernism is a throw-away word that means everything, and nothing."[10] He is right, but its lack of definition does not make it any less important.

While this dismisses postmodernity, at the same time the Church became less effective and influential. Can the Church become just a "remnant" in an evil world, and like Elijah, retreat into the wilderness to pray, "I alone am left; and they seek to take my life" (1 Kings 19:10)?

Second, the Church can launch out with an aggressive attack against the evils of postmodernity to destroy its influence. Some churches, especially legalistic churches, make a continuous practice of denouncing the evils of postmodernity and/or New Age thinking. However, if the Church goes on the offensive, it must be careful that it is not attacking postmodernity

---

10. As quoted by David L. Goetz, "The Riddle of Our Postmodern Culture: What is Postmodernism? Should We Even Care?", Leadership (Winter, 1997): 53.

to save modernity (most of us are influenced by the presuppositions of the modernity more than we realize). Goetz suggests an unusual paradox that faces the Church:

> Oddly enough, with the passing of modernity, many Christians grieve as though the faith itself were passing away. To that incredible extent, the Western Church appropriated the incredible extent, the Western Church appropriated the modern worldview to such an extent that it cannot distinguish between modern thinking and Christian thinking. Instead of lamenting the passing of modernity and calling the troops to defend of what remains of that godless ideology, Christians need to see a gift that God has given to the Church with the collapse of modernity. Post modernity presents fewer barriers than modernity for evangelism, but they are different barriers. Post modernity threatens many evangelical scholars because it is new. Evangelicals have spent several centuries developing an arsenal of weapons to use against modernity. To change the playing field now seems unfair.[11]

Third, the Church can adopt postmodernity, and like some Christian philosophers or apologists, embrace postmodernity to create a new Christianity in the image of postmodernity. That means the new "postmodern" church adopts the meaning of the new words to explain the Gospel, adapts to the principles to the church, and adapts preaching to the tolerant thinking its audience. The "postmodern church" abandons the universal truth claims of Christ.

The fourth strategy—what we suggest—is to focus evangelism on the scriptures and the Great Commission with a view of presenting the true Church to all people. This means we must recognize that the collapse of many local churches is not a bad or alarming event. Some churches deserve to die because they have abandoned New Testament "churchness." The advancement of postmodernity will not contribute to the collapse of the true Church, but will contribute to the collapse of many apostate churches or dead churches (including apostate denominations), and at the same time create the existence of a new kind of apostate church. This

---

11. Harry L. Poe, "Making the Most of Post modernity," Journal of the Academy for Evangelism (vol. 13, 1997-1998): 67.

fourth strategy suggests revival[12] is the best course of evangelism, perhaps the only course.

Every church leader seems to have a suggestion how to reach the postmodern. Warren Bird and I (Elmer) wrote a book entitled, *Into The Future: Turning Today's Church Trends into Tomorrow's Opportunities*.[13] This is a book I affectionately called, "The book of 14 piles." Bird and I examined the writings of Every church leader seems to have a suggestion how to reach the postmodern. Warren Bird and I (Elmer) wrote a book entitled, Into The Future: Turning Today's Church Trends into Tomorrow's Opportunities. This is a book I affectionately called, "The book of 14 piles." Bird and I examined the writings of approximately 100 different writers who each made a solid suggestion of what the future Church should do and become. We found there were 14 general hypotheses for suggested ministry.[14] Then I sat on my living room floor and put each book into

---

12. Revival is described as God pouring out His Spirit on His people, i.e., "I will pour out My Spirit on all flesh" (Acts 2:17). This suggests only God can rescue His Church. See Elmer L. Towns and Douglas Porter, The Ten Greatest Revivals Ever (Ann Arbor, MI: Servant Publications, 2000).

13. Elmer Towns and Warren Bird, Into the Future: Turning Today's Church Trends into Tomorrow's Opportunities (Grand Rapids: Revell, 2000).

14. Chapter One-Get Help Becoming More Healthy: ⊠Trend #1. Christians are moving away from a numbers-driven or church growth emphasis to focus on growing healthy churches; Chapter Two-Keep the Bible in One Hand and a Cup of Cold Water in the Other: ⊠Trend #2. A significant number of churches are becoming unapologetic about showing social concern without losing sight of the gospel; Chapter Three-Enter the World of Cheers, Friends, and Seinfeld: ⊠Trend #3. People today typically learn best and are reached best through multisensory and relational frameworks; Chapter Four-Learn the Language That Connects with Postmoderns: ⊠Trend #4. People today show interest in the truth of the gospel only after they've seen the relevance of the church and the credibility of Christians; Chapter Five-Turn On Your Daytime Running Lights: ⊠Trend #5. Congregations of all sizes are learning that it's better to do a few things well, rather than try to be "everything" to "everybody." As a result they are more intentionally targeted in how they position themselves; Chapter Six-Set Benchmarks for Reaching the Unchurched: ⊠Trend #6. One of the most distinctive marks of certain churches today is their ability to find and reach unchurched people. As a result, an increasing number of churches are identifying new benchmarks for measuring evangelistic success; Chapter Seven-Make More Room for Truth: ⊠Trend #7. Today's generation is the first to grow up with virtually no "public square" connection to its Judeo-Christian roots, and the next generation will be raised in North America's most secularized culture since the Pilgrims landed; Chapter Eight-Go Confidently to Mars Hill: ⊠Trend #8. Today's church is birthing a new generation of apologists, intellectuals, and scientists who are both rigorously academic and unabashedly Christian; Chapter Nine-Maximize the Strong Points of Your Worship Service: ⊠Trend #9. Worship styles in the future will be more diverse, with broader acceptance of the idea that one worship style doesn't have to fit all congregations; Chapter Ten-Cash In on Two Millennia of Good Ideas: ⊠Trend #10. Christians increasingly want to participate in worship as an experience. Many appreciate feeling connected with the two-thousand year stream of church history by the use of liturgical worship elements; Chapter Eleven-Learn to Be a Leader-Maker: ⊠Trend #11. After centuries of lip service to the "priesthood of all believers," the era has arrived when the people of God are truly becoming ministers; Chapter Twelve-Look Underneath the Megachurch Movement: ⊠Trend #12. Large churches are learning to operate at maximum impact and to be healthy by becoming the "biggest little church around;" Chapter

its appropriate pile; hence, 14 piles of books about the future of Church ministry. Then I said facetiously, "If you read this book, you don't have to read the other 100 books."

What can we learn from all of this? Many voices are telling the Church how it can meet the challenge of postmodernity. The challenge in today's world is two fold: how far should we go and what do we do when others go too far? The first part of the book address how far we should go.

To Take Away

Culture has changed, including the way people think and arrive at conclusions. People have different goals, attitudes and reasons for living. The Church can't use yesterday's methods in today's changing world and expect to be in ministry tomorrow. It's a different world; let's go meet the challenge! We do that by being the church in a different world. Let's review some key issues about what that different world looks like in areas such as church, worship, music, preaching, and evangelism.

QUESTIONS TO CHEW ON

1. Is the world really changing or is it just the perception of Christians that's changing?

2. What have Christians done in the past when their methods change? What can we learn from the way they adjusted?

3. Describe some ways Christians have gone too far to reach and win postmoderns to Christ. Why have they gone too far?

4. How have some Christians watered down doctrine to reach people in the world today? Principles? Convictions of godliness?

Thirteen-Make the Church Better Than a Business: ⊠Trend #13. Church leaders, while continuing to find valid help from secular management insights, are rediscovering the uniqueness of a church's spiritual resources and eternal mission; Chapter Fourteen-Free People to Give from the Heart: ⊠Trend #14. People will not give money because of emotional appeal or fund-raising emphasis, so much as in direct proportion to the benefit they're receiving from it, the confidence they have in its use, and the training they have received in Biblical stewardship.

5. Describe a situation where Christians have not been able to reach someone because they were hanging on to past traditions or old methods. What could they have done to be a more effective evangelist?

6. Of the four strategies to reach postmoderns suggested in this chapter, which one will your local church most likely adopt? Why? What should you do about it?

Chapter 10

THE PERIMETER OF TRUTH

The Parable

The missionaries noticed a change in the Nimo village. Before they became Christians, they boarded up their houses at night to sleep in darkness. Now, they kept a fire burning all night. The Nimo couldn't verbalize their feelings, but they felt comfortable within the light.

They built a big fire each evening when they met to sing loudly their Christians songs. Before, they worshipped idols in darkness; it was also under the cover of darkness that they fornicated, murdered and stole.

The Nimo needed the fire to see one another when they testified. Without knowing why, they came to stand by the fire when they told what Jesus had done for them. They had learned a new word "AMEN," a word they shouted often and loudly. Because the fire was the center of their fellowship, everyone wanted to get as close to it as possible, without being burned. It was only after the Nimo became a practicing church that the older ones noticed that those who were not as dedicated to Jesus would sit out on the edges of the light.

One evening came when two Nimo didn't come to the evening fire for singing and fellowship. They had been sitting on the outer perimeter of the light. Now they had gone into the darkness. The Nimo Christians prayed for them and wondered how they could get their brothers back into the light.

Because the light was where they sang, testified and memorized chapters of the Bible, they kept the fire burning all evening. Different men took turns keeping wood piled on the flames. The light became the focus of their fellowship. Those who came regularly to the light were those who were sincerely following Jesus.

Does the light do anything for those who are far away? Yes! The light—even though miles away—can do several things for those who live in darkness. First, it tells them where the light is located. Those in the darkness can see the fire; it stands out against the darkness. But there's a second thing, the light can guide a person to its source. When a person in the darkness sees the light, they know in what direction to go to get the benefits of the light. They know where to go so they can read, and where they can get warmth. If there are predators threatening to kill them, they can run to the light. There is safety within the perimeter of light.

The Bible indicates Jesus is a "light to those who walk in darkness" (Isa. 9:2, author's translation). Again, it tells us, "He is the light that lights every man that comes into the world" (John 1:9). That doesn't mean every person is redeemed. No! It means they can see the light far off. They know that God is the light of salvation, but that doesn't mean they have light. Jesus is their light shining in a dark sinful world. They must walk toward the light. They must enter through the edge into the circle of light—to get spiritual eyes to see how to walk—to get the warm fellowship of the light—to be able to see spiritual things. They only get protection within the perimeter of light.

Those outside the edge can see the light, but for some reason—for many reasons—they refuse to come to the light. For some it's their sin, "Men loved darkness, rather than light because their deeds are evil" (John 3:19). Some let their family, or job, or addiction keep them away. Some will not come to the light because of false religions, they think Buddah or the gods of Hinduism will save them. "Salvation is found in no one else, for there is no other name under heaven given to men by which we must be saved." (Acts 4:12).

Boundaries or Perimeters?

The Bible teaches there is no gray zone in a person's threshold to God. They either believe, or they don't. They either accept Jesus as their Savior, or they don't. There's no such thing as "I'm half saved," or "I half way believe," or "I believe one day but not the next." One's name is either in the Book of Life or it is not. It is similar to being pregnant. A woman cannot be half pregnant or have a mild case of pregnancy. She is pregnant or not. For those that are pregnant, it affects the entire body, mind, and soul. It captures every thought. So it is with being a Christian.

But wait a minute. Couldn't there be a half-way zone or a twilight zone? Can a person be right on salvation, but wrong on baptism? (Baptists believe a Presbyterian can go to Heaven, even though he/she is ignorant or disobedient about the Baptist's view of baptism). What about the gray area of lifestyle? What about the persons who put their trust in Jesus Christ, yet die in an adulterous affair? Will they go to Heaven? What about the ones who love their contemporary worship service and praise God wholeheartedly with hands lifted to Heaven, yet don't believe in the deity of Christ? Will they go to Heaven? What about those who agree with the Evangelical doctrinal statement of their church, yet have doubts about the existence of God? Will God welcome them into Heaven?

These are all difficult questions that push us to the limit. Are these people Christians? Only God knows, even when the person doesn't know. God knows their heart and when they meet the qualifications of the Bible, then they will be saved.

The problem with belief and doubt is the gray twilight zone. Compounding the problem with this gray perimeter is it differs with each individual. Some are absolutely sure about doctrine, but waver on lifestyle. Some live pure lives but have intellectual problems about doctrine. They are good with obedience but not good with thinking things out. And then there is the person who's all heart but not much head. He loves God with all his heart, but don't ask him to do a lot of thinking. How much knowledge is needed for salvation?

So, one person jumps over an emotional fence, while another quickly jumps over an intellectual fence. A third person has difficulty with making choices and self-discipline. They have a weak will. When someone has difficulty with one of these fences, does that mean there are different fences that give problems to different people? Maybe the fences are located at different places in their heart.

So, when you look inside the conversion experience of different believers, does it mean there is a hard fence (boundary) to jump over into Heaven, or that there is only a perimeter between light and darkness?

The perimeter between light and darkness can be different to different people if they have differing eyesight. Suppose one is far-sighted and they think they must go much farther to read in the light than average sighted people. Suppose some are near-sighted. Can they think they are in the light when they are not?

These questions are asked to demonstrate that some walk out of darkness into light much sooner and much easier than others. Again we suggest the boundary between the lost and saved is not a fence; it's a perimeter of light.

The problem with understanding the perimeter of light is the issue of shadows. When you are walking toward the light, the shadows are behind you. You don't see them and they don't bother you if you are walking straight toward Jesus.

What about the person who tries to sneak into the perimeter of light? They see pure light but they don't face Jesus; they face the shadows. Could these shadows be the doubts they have about some doctrine? Or doubts about their ability to live for Jesus? Or about what some other Christian has done to them?

The closer you get to Jesus—the light—the less threatening the shadows. So those who walk through the perimeter of light will see their doubts begin to go away as they get closer to Jesus. How close must they get to be completely in the edge? They must be born again. How close must they get—to eliminate their shadows—before they are converted?

Is it possible to be dragged through the perimeter of light into salvation? John Warwick Montgomery claims he was dragged "kicking and screaming" into the Kingdom.[1] In the book, A Severe Mercy, author Sheldon Vanauken continued to argue with C. S. Lewis against the existence of God and spiritual things. When C. S. Lewis answered all his questions, Vanauken said, "I could no longer doubt, I could no longer be an unbeliever."[2] This is called the argument of congruity, i.e., when your questions are answered, you can no longer doubt. But does that mean the person has New Testament faith? Is it possible to be dragged all the way into the light—to Jesus—to be saved?

Then there are some who are born within the perimeter of light. Their parents are Christian and they are brought up in a Christian church. They think they are Christians, but have never made a decision for Christ. Outwardly they live a Christian life, but something happens—sickness, failure, or loss of hope—they turn against the Church and deny the light in which they were born and raised. They quit trying to do things in the Church.

---

1. Dr. Montgomery is a personal friend of Elmer Towns and in giving his testimony, Dr. Montgomery related this incident.
2. Sheldon Vanauken, A Severe Mercy (San Francisco: Harper, 1992), n.p.

Putting their back to the light, they walk away. With the light behind them, they see shadows . . . threatening shadows . . . ominous shadows . . . shadows blacker than they have ever seen in life. Outside the light, shadows grow larger as doubts become greater.

Questions

When you look for the perimeter between light and darkness, it's hard to see. When you stand in the light and look toward the darkness, it seems the light doesn't penetrate very far into the darkness. Maybe it's the perspective. You tend to see things well if they are close and you have difficulty seeing things far away. And since you can't see an actual edge, you think it's in the distance.

What about the perimeter? Where is it? If you're standing outside the light, you think it's a long way off. You can see the light and you know what light is. But when you're walking towards the light, it seems the perimeter—like the horizon—keeps moving away from you.

As you walk toward the light, you enter a twilight zone that's neither full light nor full darkness. Everything appears fuzzy. You can see things, but not clearly, but you can see well while you're in the light. But you also know there's more light in front of you. If you want to see more clearly, you'll need to get closer to the light. When you walk in the twilight, you don't think you're in either the light or in the darkness, but you're really in darkness.

The twilight zone appears to be on the outside of the perimeter of light. You step through the perimeter of light to walk in semi-darkness. If you were in the light, you'd be aware of some changes in perception. Your eyes would begin to dilate and things would become clearer. It's good when a person's ability to perceive things is in harmony with the amount of available light. Then you're able to see . . . to read . . . and to properly go about your business. You have light to live for God. Then you enjoy the protection and comfort that you have from the fire.

Five Perimeters

This chapter will examine five perimeters of Christianity, i.e., five perimeters of light. It is always difficult to draw perimeters. The task has been attempted before—and has been controversial every time. Our intent here is not to cause controversy but to suggest perimeters. Today, this issue is on the mind of evangelicals. The Evangelical Theological Society just this year argued about the boundaries (confronting open theism), and appropriately so. Recently, an excellent book tried to convey what evangelicals believe in *This We Believe*[3] (signed by hundreds of evangelical leaders). Our intent here is not to set forth the technical theological issues (though they are important), but to provide suggestions for evaluation about that perimeter of Christianity.

The Five Perimeters of Christianity
1. Jesus.
2. The Gospel.
3. Bible doctrine.
4. Christian experience.
5. God's blessing.

The following perimeters, with their implied limits, do not conflict in God's mind, only in our understanding of what God said. Because none of us has all the facts on which to make decisions and none has perfect reasoning faculties to understand perfectly, and none of us has a broad background to experience all that God is doing; the edge may get fuzzy sometimes, while at other times everything is clear. This chapter will attempt to help us clarify God's perimeters our belief and ministry.

PERIMETER ONE—JESUS: Essential Christianity recognizes the biblical person of Jesus Christ as the core for its belief and practice.

Christianity is Jesus Christ and those who come to God must come by Him (John 14:6). Jesus is the revelation of the Father to the world. Those who believe in Christianity must believe in Him (John 1:12) and those who preach Christianity, must preach Him (Acts 4:12).

But when is the preaching of Jesus not an effective communication of Christianity? Is the message of Jesus Christ presented in many Roman Catholic sermons and writings adequate to save a hearer? (They demand works for salvation). What about the story of Jesus in the Qur'an or the Book of Mormon? Will that message save? (They present Jesus as an historical person). Will the message of Jesus in a Hollywood movie save a hearer? Can the message of a glamorized Jesus that includes His death

---

3. Akers, J. K., John H. Armstrong, and John D. Woodbridge, eds. *This We Believe: The Good News of Jesus Christ for the World* (Grand Rapids: Zondervan Publishing House, 2000).

on the cross save? (The first part of the question deals with the subjective intent of the presenter; the second asks if there is enough objective content to save?).

How much about Jesus must a person know to be saved? His sinless life? His miracles? His deity? His substitutionary death? Besides the complete message of the Gospel, how accurate must the presentation be?

What do you have to believe about Jesus to be saved? Obviously, you have to believe that His death provides the forgiveness of your sins. The Bible teaches, "Without the shedding of blood there is no forgiveness of sin" (Heb. 9:22). The Bible also teaches that you have to believe that Jesus is Lord (Romans 10:9) in order to be saved. Can you believe Jesus sinned yet died for your sins?

Suppose another person believes each individual must determine what religion is good for him and that all religions lead to God, yet this person prays to accept Jesus as Savior. In addition to his relationship with Jesus he consults a horoscope for everyday living. Will that person go to Heaven if he believes Jesus is only one way to Heaven?

What is the problem with these two people? If the light flickers low—the person has false information—can he or she still be safe by entering within the *perimeter of light*? How much does a person have to know about Jesus to be saved? If a drowning man yells for help, all he has to do is grab the lifesaver to be rescued. He doesn't need to know the make of the lifesaver, manufacturer's specs, nor the theology of the thrower.

How much does a person have to know? The two examples may seem extreme, but they are not. Many people first professed Christ do so while in doctrinal confusion. Would anyone want to require a person to understand the intricacies of Christology before committing to follow Christ? Of course not—we believe that once a person meets Jesus, they will learn more and more about him. But how much light is required for the young child to commit her life to Christ?

What about the thief on the cross? How much "light" did he have? The unbelieving thief said, "If thou be Christ, save thyself and us" (Luke 23:39). But the believing thief rebuked him. "We indeed (die) justly . . . but this man hath done nothing amiss. And he said unto Jesus, 'Lord remember me when you come into thy kingdom'" (Luke 23:41, 42). All the repentant thief knew about Jesus was that Jesus was a just man who did nothing wrong and that Jesus was the Messiah. How did he believe? He said, "Remember me . . ." Jesus responded to him, "Verily I say unto you, today you shall be with Me in Paradise" (Luke 23:43). The perimeter of light seemed to reach very far to him.

Nicodemus had a lot of biblical knowledge, but the *perimeter of light* was drawn much tighter for him than for the thief on the cross. Nicodemus knew the Law, for Jesus called him "the teacher of Israel" (John 3:10). Nicodemus knew much about Jesus, "'Rabbi, we know you are a teacher who has come from God. For no one could perform the miraculous signs you are doing if God were not with him'" (John 3:2). Nicodemus knew all these things but was lost. Jesus told him, "You must be born again" (John 3:3, 7). Apparently a person can know so much about the Bible that the circle is very narrow for them. The perimeter of light was as narrow for Nicodemus as his understanding of the nature of the new birth.

Right after drawing the circle smaller for Nicodemus, Jesus broadens the *perimeter of light* much larger for the woman at the well. She was not blinded to the light with false doctrine or good works, as was Nicodemus; she was blinded to the light by her sin. She had been married five times, now she was living out of wedlock, i.e., in adultery. Also, she was of a different ethnic background; she was a Samaritan, Jesus was a Jew. She was looking for the Messiah (John 4:25), but believed Jesus was just a man (John 4:19). How big was her circle of light? She said, "Come, see a man who told me everything I ever did. Could this be the Christ?" (John 4:29).

What can we conclude from these illustrations of those who met the Savior?

(1) You must know Jesus, for He is the only way to the Father (John 14:6).

(2) God will stretch the circle of light to those who know only the essentials.

(3) Your sinful condition may determine how much you need to know about Christ, or at least how you will express your belief.

(4) Too much Bible knowledge without inner faith could be a barrier to belief. The circle of light is not stretched for those who do not "live or act on the light they have."

PERIMETER TWO—THE GOSPEL: Essential Christianity recognizes salvation is in the person of Jesus as accomplished in His death, burial, and resurrection.

The Jesus perimeter is not entered when the message of Jesus is inconsistent with the presentation in scripture of His person and work. The essence of Christianity is the gospel message, i.e., the good news. Theologians call this the kerygma—the fundamental message of the gospel. This message is objectively written in words, i.e., the propositional gospel, and humanly experienced in the person of Jesus Christ, i.e., the personal gospel.

The Gospel—a proposition. The basis of good news is the death, burial and resurrection of Jesus Christ. This message is best expressed in these words of Paul,

> *"Now, brothers, I want to remind you of the gospel I preached to you, which you received and on which you have taken your stand. By this gospel you are saved, if you hold firmly to the word I preached to you. Otherwise, you have believed in vain. For what I received I passed on to you as of first importance: that Christ died for our sins according to the Scriptures, that he was buried, that he was raised on the third day according to the Scriptures"* (1 Cor. 15:1-4).

The Gospel message is fundamentally the death, burial, and bodily resurrection of Jesus Christ. In His death, He forgave our sins and took them away. In His resurrection, He gives us new life, i.e., eternal life. Those who deny the reality of these truths, deny the essence of Christianity. But a person is not saved by mere mental agreement to this propositional statement. Many have had head knowledge of Jesus' death, burial and resurrection, yet were not regenerated by that proposition. It's not head knowledge that leads a person to genuine faith; it also includes heart knowledge. (A person could have correct head knowledge about a fire, but that person would get no benefits from the fire until he or she moved within the *perimeter of light*.)

This helps us to understand that embracing this light does involve some facts—facts that are recorded in a text. What do we know of Jesus except that which is recorded in the Bible? That Bible provides a proposition that is a central part of being in the light—that Jesus "came down from heaven… was incarnate of the Holy Spirit and the Virgin Mary… and became truly human… was crucified… suffered death and was buried. On the third day he rose again in accordance with the scriptures" (the Nicene Creed).

The scripture itself points to the propositional truth recorded in the words of the Bible:

> *"For what I received I passed on to you as of first importance: that Christ died for our sins according to the Scriptures, that he was buried, that he was raised on the third day according to the scriptures"* (1 Corinthians 15:3, 4).

The Gospel—a Person. The Gospel is more than a proposition, i.e., head knowledge; it is a person—Jesus Christ. Becoming a Christian involves more than giving mental assent to the fact of the death, burial and resurrection of Jesus. The gospel enters our lives when Jesus Christ enters our hearts. "But as many as received Him [Christ], to them He gave the right to become children of God, even to those who believe in His name" (John 1:12).

But when is the gospel not the gospel of Jesus Christ? Today, there is great interest in spiritual things. Barnes & Noble's spirituality section is filled with books about being spiritual, and many teach about Jesus—but this Jesus is remarkably dissimilar from the Jesus of scripture.

Communication always involves four elements: First, the **message** to be communicated; second the **source-encoder**, i.e., the person sending the message; third, the **media** or the way the message is communicated, and fourth, the **receiver-decoder**, the one receiving the message and interpreting it. All four influence the essence of communicating the gospel.

First, when the message is the same as contained in scripture, there is no problem. But some think Jesus died as my substitute, others think Jesus died only as my example of righteous suffering, still others teach a mystical element to His death; while others say His death was a mistake. How much correct doctrine must be poured into the message of the gospel?

Second, the source-encoder (the messenger) may have various meanings in his/her head when communicating the gospel. Can God use a messenger when the gospel is communicated from the point of view of a Hyper-Calvinist, Arminian, cultist, liberal, or television producer? Does the orientation of the source-encoder influence the message? Contaminate the message?

These questions lead us to the boundary, i.e., the fence. At what point does the gospel of scripture no longer remain the gospel? When have we not preached Christ? Before drawing a boundary, remember the Bible story. John wanted to keep the boundary close to his perception, and kick out anyone who didn't agree with him. The apostle said, "Master . . . we tried to stop him (from preaching), because he is not one of us." But Jesus said to him, "Do not stop him," Jesus said, "for whoever is not against you is for you" (Luke 9:48-50). Suppose a source-encoder completely misunderstands the gospel, but communicates its kerygma correctly, can God use it? Paul explained that people preach Christ for many different motives—but his concern was the gospel was preached (Philippians 1:15-18).

Third, what about the media? Is the message the media, or is the reverse true? Are there some media that can't be used to present the Gospel because the media is contaminated in the minds of the source-encoder? Receiver-decoder? (Much more on this later.)

Fourth, the receiver-decoder may be hindered by presuppositions, ignorance, blindness, prejudice, attention-disorders, etc. Is the Gospel properly communicated if the receiver-decoder doesn't understand it? Does it take two to communicate? (More on this later when we discuss evangelism.)

MISSING THE PERIMETER: The gospel perimeter is not effective when good works are attached as a condition for salvation, or the substitutionary nature of Jesus' death is not presented, or is denied, or an alternate understanding of salvation is attached to the presentation.

PERIMETER THREE—DOCTRINE: Essential Christianity recognizes the authority of Scriptures, the deity of Jesus, His substitutionary death for the forgiveness of sins, His physical resurrection to give new life and His bodily return for the consummation of His purposes on earth.

There are certain essentials of Christian truth that form the core for Christian objective doctrine. These truths were debated in the liberal-fundamentalist controversies from 1900 to 1950. These doctrinal fundamentals, like things that are essential to the operation of an automobile, are essential to Christianity. If you take an essential away from Christianity, what remains is no longer Christianity.

A car cannot be operated without tires, steering wheel, fuel, pump, etc. Without these, the car is inoperative. A car is not a car if it doesn't have a motor, but it can still be a car if it doesn't have a glove box, backseat or trunk. Without certain essential doctrines, Christianity is inoperative. This means when you take certain Christian doctrines out of Christianity, it is no longer Christianity. Following the analogy, what core doctrines are essential to Christianity?

First is the authority and perfection of scripture as the revelation of God's person and will. Take away the authority of the Bible, or the essential content of the Bible, and you no longer have Christianity.

Second is the deity of Jesus Christ, God who was born of a virgin to become fully man, and man who is fully God. Take away the truth of His virgin birth and you no longer have Christianity.

Third is the substitutionary atonement of Jesus Christ for sins, as evidence in the shedding of His blood. If forgiveness of sins by the blood is missing from the message, it is not Christianity.

Fourth is the physical resurrection of Jesus Christ from death to give us new life; and fifth is the bodily return of Jesus Christ to take His children to live with Him and to judge those who reject His plan of salvation.

Some would deny there is a theological boundary or doctrinal perimeter to Christianity; they would suggest that the only requirement of Christianity is to believe Jesus and accept the gospel. Although this belief would make one a Christian, it is not enough to define the belief system as Christianity.

Christianity affirms the Trinitarian existence of God the Father, God the Son and God the Holy Spirit. Christianity affirms certain beliefs or doctrines. That is what defines this faith called Christianity.

It may take less doctrine to become a Christian, but it does take more doctrine to be Christianity. How much can be denied and still retain the essentials of Christianity? To the authors, the essentials of Christianity are wrapped up in the Apostle's Creed:

The Apostles Creed

> "I believe in God the Father Almighty, maker of heaven and earth; and in Jesus Christ His only Son, our Lord; who was conceived by the Holy Spirit, born of the Virgin Mary, suffered under Pontius Pilate, was crucified, dead, and buried; He descended into Hades; the third day He rose again from the dead; He ascended into heaven, and sitteth on the right hand of God, the Father Almighty; from thence He shall come to judge the quick and the dead. I believe in the Holy Spirit, the holy Christian church, the communion of saints, the forgiveness of sins, the resurrection of the body, and life everlasting. Amen."

Anyone who denies "the doctrine of Christ" has questioned His Sonship, His virgin birth, His atoning death and His resurrection. John suggests,

> "Anyone who runs ahead and does not continue in the teaching of Christ does not have God; whoever continues in the teaching has both the Father and the Son" (2 John 9).

> "No one who denies the Son has the Father; whoever acknowledges the Son has the Father also" (1 John 2:23).

Thus, there is a perimeter of light where a church or denomination is no longer Christian, but something else. There may be Christians within that group, but that group is no longer Christian. It may sound harsh, but it is not intended to be so. However, we must ask—what makes the beliefs Christian and what is beyond the perimeter of the light?

Both of the authors are Baptists, yet we would not say that Presbyterians are outside the light; even though we believe that they have misunderstood some teachings about baptism (we assume our Presbyterians brothers feel the same about us!). Yet, there are some groups that cannot meet the test described above—they have gone beyond the edge or are founded outside of that boundary.

In some cases, these are churches and denominations that were once biblically faithful and today have walked away and beyond the realm of the light. They have denied the biblical doctrines above and have become apostate. They have gone to the edge and fallen off—in this case into liberalism. They can no longer be called Christian.

On the other hand, there are some aberrant groups that have denied the fundamentals. By their founding, they have placed themselves outside of the light by denying the deity of Christ, or the Trinity, etc. They never were in the light.

Although there may be Christians in these groups, these groups are outside of the perimeter of the light—they are not Christianity. Yet, many Christians disagree on certain doctrinal manners—and are still within the perimeter of light.

MISSING THE PERIMETER: The doctrinal edge is not effective when the essential belief of Christianity is not presented, or is denied, or an opposite belief is presented.

PERIMETER FOUR-- CHRISTIAN EXPEREINCE: Essential Christianity recognizes that the experience of saving faith will

produce forgiveness, cleansing of sins, and assurance of one's relationship with God. The experience of continued faith will produce the positive fruits of the Spirit and a desire to serve the indwelling Christ.

The child of God has unique experiences that are not shared with other religions, nor with other faith groups, i.e., those historically identified as cults or world religions. The Christian experience begins when a person believes the gospel (propositional truth) and receives Jesus (personal truth).

The personal act of faith is an experience that is based on the objective statement of the faith. This experience changes those who believe in Jesus Christ. Jesus Christ lives in their life (Gal. 2:20), they are motivated as they experience God's love, God's grace, and God's peace. They give evidence of the fruit of the Spirit (Gal. 5:22, 23), and they receive confidence in their relationship to God (1 John 5:11-13).

There are many ways to clarify the perimeters of Christian experience. First, Christianity is not a religion; it is a relationship. Therefore, Christians are not people who have adopted the moral code and rules of Christ; they are people who have met Jesus. They have met him and committed their lives to him—this is their Christian experience.

This experience differs drastically from Christian to Christian. Sometimes Christians say, "I have no testimony." They explain that they never lived a tremendously immoral life and thus, they can tell no great story of conversion. However, they misunderstand what a testimony is. A testimony is when one testifies about a relationship. Every true Christian must be able to tell about that relationship.

For some, that will involve walking an aisle at a church service; others will start the relationship reading the Bible in a hotel room; still others will start that relationship after a long intellectual search. However, fundamental to that experience is that there is an introduction—a person becomes a Christian, he or she is not born one. The Bible says that their name is written in the book of life, it was not there at birth.

When a person claims to be a Christian, but does not have any Christian experience, or at least some of the experiences of Christianity, that person's faith is not yet complete. They have head knowledge, but that is not enough. They must pass from death to life, from darkness to light.

That experience is then followed by a changed life—also an experience. The experience leads to another experience, i. e., the Christian life.

While the world may deny or mock the Christian experience, it's an experience that is real to those who have it. It's the difference between walking in darkness and walking in light. If you've been in the black night, you know the experience of light. Listen to the blind man testify to his new experience, "Once I was blind, now I see" (John 9:25).

MISSING THE PERIMETER: The Christian experience edge is not effective when the empirical results (life change) that should follow salvation are denied, or the opposite is taught by those offering salvation.

PERIMETER FIVE–THE BLESSABILITY CORE: Blessability is the presence of God in the life of those who follow biblical criteria by serving the Lord; by exercising hope (in the future work of God), faith (in the ability of God to do what He promised), and love (deep feelings of compassion for those to whom ministry is given). God's blessing is evident in His power to transform, motivate, deliver, and give abundant life to followers.

Over the years we have witnessed the blessing of God on various groups, i.e., both Calvinists and Arminians, both charismatics and cessationists, both high church and low church, both those who sprinkle and immerse, both liturgical and contemporary praise worship services, both teetotalers and "sippers," both fundamentalists and moderates. But as we observe the blessing of God in ministry, it is important to ask some central questions:

1. How can God bless people on both sides of a disagreement, when one obviously is wrong?

2. Obviously there is an outer perimeter of God's blessing. What is the least essential belief that a person must embrace to experience God's blessing?

3. Why was God not more explicit to explain the outer perimeters or boundary of Christianity?

4. Obviously, God blesses certain non-tangibles that are not involved with these issues. What are the non-tangibles that God blesses?

The blessing of God is similar in definition to atmospheric worship or atmospheric revival, i.e., "The presence of God among his people." Revival is defined, "I will pour out My Spirit" (Joel 2:29). It is also described, "When times of refreshing shall come from the presence of the Lord" (Acts 3:19). The blessing of God is not bigger crowds, big responses at the altar, growth in membership, offerings, baptisms, etc. The blessing of God is an intangible experience of God evidently working in the hearts of listeners as the gospel is preached. The blessing of God is when He gives His presence to the thing, event or person who is blessed. The blessing of God results in experiential Christianity, but it is based on objective truth, i.e., the gospel, essential doctrine, Jesus, and Christian experiences.

There are many problems when using the blessability of God as criteria for the edge of Christianity. First, the blessing of God is similar to being used by God. There were some obvious illustrations of ungodly people that God used, i.e., Pharaoh (Rom. 9:17) and Cyrus (Is. 45:1). Sometimes God may use the communication of the gospel message by unsaved persons; He may even use a person who is anti-Christian to communicate the Gospel to lost people. But being used of God does not mean they have the blessing of God, i.e., they enjoy the presence of God in their life or they enjoy Christian experiences in their life. So there may be a difference between the Christians we accept and endorse, and those who claim to be Christian, but we reject them as true believers.

A second problem with the blessibility criteria is that groups outside of Christianity seem to be "blessed." If one of the blessings of God is growth, would we say that the Jehovah's Witnesses are blessed of God? Since they deny many of the basic tenants of right doctrine, we cannot call their growth a blessing of God. We cannot call the Mormon wealth a blessing of God. Outward blessing is not enough to be called a Christian blessing.

When God blesses a person we need to ask, "What is He blessing?" Is God blessing the person's spiritual gifts? Her prayer ministry? His preparation? Her spirituality? Sometimes God is not blessing or using the person at all. God is blessing the message of the gospel or the Word of God. God's blessing doesn't rest on the one communicating the message.

Some people are more focused on what they won't do, rather than what they will do. They are more focused on what they are against, than what they support. They may oppose another pastor's doctrine, lifestyle, or worship expression but God may be blessing the one they oppose. But what does God bless? Does God bless the gift He originally gave the person, or does God bless the gospel content (i.e., the message of a sermon), and not put His blessing on the minister (i.e., the messenger)?

Because our emotions and feelings are both fleeting and misleading, John tells us to "test the Spirits" (1 John 4:1). We can deceive ourselves and deceive others. We must test our feeling—and the blessing of God—by doctrine (1 John 4:2-3). Paul tells us to get the big picture, "Test everything. Hold on to the good" (1 Thess. 5:21). Right foundational beliefs combined with the blessability of God are clear evidence of being within the perimeter of the light.

MISSING THE PERIMETER: The blessability edge is not effective when the presence of God as reflected in scriptures is denied, or those claiming God's presence teach the opposite.

TO TAKE AWAY

We have many friends in denominations that hold beliefs that are different than ours, but we agree on the essential core of doctrine. With them, there is so much more doctrinal agreement than disagreement. Nevertheless, because we are all within the perimeters of Christianity, "we be brethren."

In essentials, unity.

In non-essentials, tolerance.

In all things, love.

We have many friends who have different standards from us for Christian living and practices of holiness. We do not think we are better than they, and if they are willing to tolerate our personal Christian life-style, "we be brethren."

Elmer began his Christian life in a Presbyterian church and Ed in an Episcopal church; Elmer graduated from two Methodist institutions of higher education, plus two seminaries that would be classified Independent. Ed has graduated from four Baptist schools and one that would be considered Interdenominational. Today we minister in Baptist churches but our greatest allegiance is to Jesus Christ. If that is your allegiance, then "we be brethren."

QUESTIONS TO CHEW ON

1. When a person starts believing in Jesus as a historic person but has not had a personal conversion experience, how close are they to the perimeter of salvation?

2. How far away from Christ does a person have to walk before they are no longer considered within the perimeter of light?

3. How much of the gospel must a person know to be saved?

4. Is it possible for a person to outwardly live the Christian experience and walk in the perimeter of light, yet not be born again?

5. If blessibility is an edge of the light, how much blessing must a person have to be within the perimeter of light?

6. How much false doctrine can you tolerate with a spirit of Christian love? When must you disagree?

Epilogue

Again, take your position high above the night jungle. Look in every direction; you'll see flickering lights in the night. Some tiny lights may be individuals who carry light away from our two fictional missionaries. As the light travels through the night, it stops; then enlightens the surrounding area. The new light may be a converted family, or a house church.

Sometimes you'll see a larger glow in the darkness, a glow from several individual lights making one larger light. When a tribe has been converted, each individual carrying a light spreads their influence so an entire home or street or neighborhood is illuminated.

Within the perimeter of the enlightened towns, nightwalkers get the benefit of the light; they're warm, they're protected, so when they live in the light they have better lives. The light from light-bearers has made them happier and healthier. This means the influence of Christianity has benefited all who live within the reach of light.

As you survey the dark horizon, you'll notice pools of light coming together so that there are some larger illuminated areas. People who live in these areas don't have to take light with them wherever they go; they benefit from other light-bearers.

When the pools of light get bigger and brighter, Christians seem happy. They feel victorious to be on a winning side that's conquering darkness. There have been times in history where light was on the march, i.e., the apostolic church, the Reformation, the First-Century awakening, the missionary thrust of the 18th century, etc.

But from your lofty position above the jungle, notice some large pools of light that seem to be dimming. And then you notice some individual torches flickering low. You can even see some red embers of ashes that used to be a roaring fire. In some places the darkness is winning individuals and some churches are succumbing to the onslaught of night. When Christians seek darkness more than light, the torch of their good deeds goes out.

The jungle is made up of light and darkness, each opposed to the other; each dedicated to the elimination of the other. Who's going to win? The one that does the best job. If the light shines brightly, it will penetrate the night to capture those in the darkness. When the light is light, it can push back the darkness. We know that ultimately, the light of Christ will overcome the light of darkness… but a lot of unbelievers will live and die in darkness before that final victory.

However, the darkness is relentless, like a starving predator; the night will always tempt light-bearers into its domain. If light-holders would simply hold high their light, darkness could not threaten them.

Today, the American church is under attack. It's trying desperately to hold on to the territory it previously won from the darkness. But, light can't hold on to light and at the same time flirt with the darkness. Will darkness teach us how to make a fire? Can the night enlighten others? Can the world show us how to evangelize? Can we blindly use the world's methods to worship? To evangelize? To live holy lives?

Obviously, we would answer "no" to all these questions, and rightly so. Yet, our task is not just the rejection of culture, but we must take the light to each setting. Thus, we bring the light to a new village in the jungle—one with different traditions, music, dress, etc. The light is not extinguished, but instead, it redeems that which it touches. The light gives us the clarity to decide what can and what cannot be used. The light both gives us ability to see and turns what was dark into that which is light. The light is both informative and transformative—it shows us that is appropriate and redeems some things to make them appropriate.

As you look down on the few islands of light in an otherwise black jungle, do you see shadows? Some shadows extend from pure light into the territory of darkness? However, people in the darkness are not hurrying to the light. It's hard for people in the night to know what to do where there are so many shadows in their life. They can't walk safely in shadows, nor can they walk confidently. They don't know where to go. They stumble in shadows, hurting themselves; or even worse, they die in the shadows when light is close by.

But look again from your position above the jungle, shadows also dance closer to the fire. It's not the people of the dark who are threatened by shadows; it's people of the light. A shadow close to a fire can cause a light-walker to stumble. They don't have to be in darkness to stumble. Isn't there some faulty worship or marginal preaching right next to the fire?

We would wish that we would never have to ask, "When is biblical preaching no longer biblical?" We should not have to struggle with the issue, "When is worship no longer worship?" and "When is Christian music no longer Christian?" Instead of ministering in the perimeter of light, we should attempt to serve as close to the light as possible. The light is the key—we are to let the light of scripture and the illumination of the Holy Spirit help us to determine what it the right method or approach.

However, this book is about both the gospel (light) and unredeemed culture (darkness). We must know the light and let it transform our lives. Then, we must know where darkness is located, so we can take the light to it. We must understand culture to know the best methods to shine light on its dark corners.

The message of this book is that perimeters of light are dangerous when the damp night air is putting out the light. However, balance that negative with a positive perspective. The perimeters are good when we're pushing them into the night, when we're conquering its territory and when we're illuminating more night-dwellers. The light is being light when it is informing us about, and then transforming, the darkness.

We hold the light with a great humility. We know that WE are not the light, but the light is from God and is found in His Word and through his Spirit. So our task is to show people the light and trust the light to do its work. Sometimes, we want to be the light and tell every culture, people, and generation that this is the only way things must be done. We have seen in this book that this will not work.

Instead, light by its very nature, goes everywhere—informing and transforming. We are to give away the light so it might inform and transform other cultures and generations. Instead of thinking we are the source of the light, we give it away—and let it do what it does best. Certainly, we can help inform new believers in a postmodern age about what the light has done for us—but we also must recognize that we end up in a three way conversation, rather than a two way conversation. We are not just giving them the light, we are introducing them to a new relationship.

This might be best illustrated as follows. Our task is to boldly take the unchanging light, but to recognize that it is the light that matters, and not how it has illuminated my world.

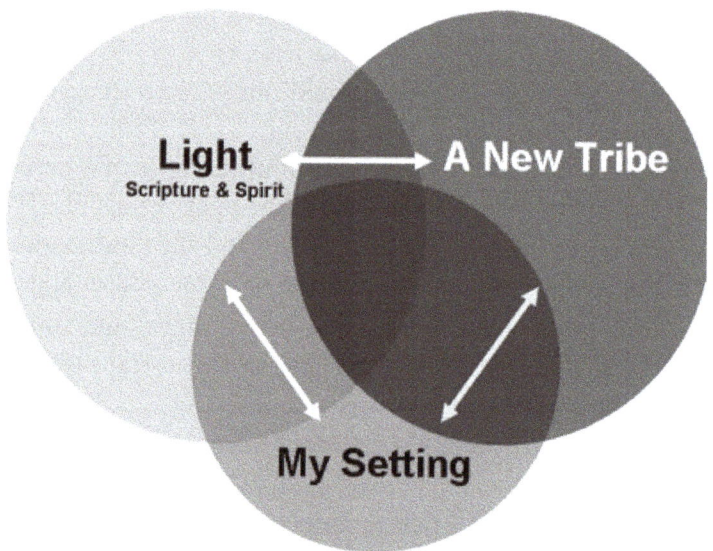

What we end up with is a church and a Christian that is faithful to the scriptures and living the light in its own community. What was once a dark jungle has become a new expression of the light. It has become a missional church—a new mission outpost in what was once a dark jungle of lostness.

May you take the light with you allowing you it to inform and transform your world. May we also be wise enough to allow it to inform and transform the lives and worlds of others. Most importantly, may we remember that the light does not change, but where and how it is expressed does. Our expressions of church, preaching, worship, and are not the center of the perimeter of light. God is. He has shed his light in the early church, in the middle ages, in the reformation, in the missionary movements, in the great awakenings and renewals, and He will shed His light in thie emerging postmodern world. Sure, it will look different, but the light remains the same.

"The people who walk in darkness will see a great light—a light that will shine on all who live in the land where death casts its shadow" (Is. 9:2, NLT).

"Jesus said to the people, 'I am the light of the world. If you follow me, you won't be stumbling through the darkness, because you will have the light that leads to life'" (John 8:12, NLT).

Send the light, the blessed gospel light…

BOOKS BY ELMER L. TOWNS

Dare to Love

How God Answers Prayers

Knowing God Through Fasting

Praying Genesis

Praying for Your Job

Praying For Your Second Chance: Prayers from Numbers and Deuteronomy

Praying Paul's Letters

Praying the Book of Acts and the General Epistles

Praying the Book of Job

Praying the Book of Revelation

Praying the Gospels

Praying the Heart of David

Praying the New Testament

Praying the Proverbs, Song of Solomon, and Ecclesiastes

Praying the Psalms

Praying With The Conquerors: Prayers from Joshua, Judges, and Ruth

Praying Your Way Out of Bondage: Prayers from Exodus and Leviticus

AVAILABLE FROM DESTINY IMAGE PUBLISHERS

FREE E-BOOKS?
YES, PLEASE!

Get **FREE** and deeply discounted **Christian books** for your **e-reader** delivered to your inbox **every week!**

IT'S SIMPLE!

VISIT lovetoreadclub.com

SUBSCRIBE by entering your email address

RECEIVE free and discounted e-book offers and inspiring articles delivered to your inbox every week!

Unsubscribe at any time.

SUBSCRIBE NOW!

LOVE TO READ CLUB

visit **LOVETOREADCLUB.COM** ▶

www.ingramcontent.com/pod-product-compliance
Ingram Content Group UK Ltd.
Pitfield, Milton Keynes, MK11 3LW, UK
UKHW022225230426
12048UKWH00016BA/1076